WHY IS
THAT
IN THE
BIBLE?

THE **MOST PERPLEXING** VERSES AND STORIES
—AND WHAT THEY TEACH US

Eric J. Bargerhuff

BETHANYHOUSE
a division of Baker Publishing Group
Minneapolis, Minnesota

Published by Bethany House Publishers
11400 Hampshire Avenue South
Bloomington, Minnesota 55438
www.bethanyhouse.com

Bethany House Publishers is a division of
Baker Publishing Group, Grand Rapids, Michigan

Printed in the United States of America

ISBN 978-0-7642-3399-9

Library of Congress Control Number: 2019059820

Cover design by Rob Williams, InsideOutCreativeArts

20   21   22   23   24   25   26   7   6   5   4   3   2   1

With each season of life, people cross your path who you know have been strategically placed there by the LORD. Two men come to mind as recent sources of encouragement, prayer, and support: Dr. James Gills and Dr. Dennis Cox. Their genuine love for the LORD and for people has had an impact on so many, and I am privileged to count myself as one of those who have received the blessings that their service to God brings.

Thank you, men, for the role you have played
in my spiritual journey.

Contents

Introduction

Perhaps the most shocking verse in the Bible is Job 1:8, where the LORD says to Satan, "Have you considered my servant Job?"—essentially offering up a godly man for a season of unprecedented testing and anguish. The story is an astounding account of a man who is faithfully walking with the LORD, and then sees his livestock, servants, even his children, perish in the blink of an eye. Not only that, but Job's health takes a turn for the worse, his wife opposes him, and his closest friends show up with rampant speculations and bad advice. Only toward the end of his life does the situation drastically change.

Job's story is the antidote to the "prosperity gospel" of our time, the belief that if you simply have enough faith, then physical, material, or financial blessings will undoubtedly be God's will for you. Yet the fact that the LORD allowed Satan to inflict devastating blows to Job's life (but put limits on what he could do) demonstrates to us that God is sovereign over all of life, both good times and bad, and that material blessings of all kinds are not a measure of one's faith. God is worthy of being worshiped and trusted even if what happens to us remains a mystery.

I, for one, am so thankful this story is in the Bible. I believe it is there to teach us many lessons, one being that things happen in the heavenly realms that we are not always privy to when we go through seasons of suffering. Another lesson is that sometimes our suffering is directly related to our lifestyle, and other times it is not. Either way, in Job's story we get a needed perspective of the heavenly realms.

Through the course of this book, we will look at some of the most perplexing verses and stories in the Bible. We are limited in what we can cover space-wise, so I have done my best to present a healthy cross section of passages—the strange, the disgusting, the controversial, the mysterious, and the flat-out hard to believe—all for the purpose of asking, *Why is* that *in the Bible?*

Some of these stories and verses are difficult to interpret, so I include a concise summary and simple interpretation of each, using a sound, scholarly interpretive approach to ancient texts. I believe there is only one proper interpretation of the Bible (in context), but several applications can be borne from the text. My method of interpretation is the literal, grammatical, historical interpretation, where the goal is to discover the original author's intent and to understand the context in which it was originally spoken, written, and heard. We should avoid allegorizing or spiritualizing texts in a way that is foreign to the original author's intent. This is how many have misused, misinterpreted, and misapplied this ancient document.

I believe the Bible is fully inspired by God and is without error in the original manuscripts. When all the facts are fully known, the Bible will be shown to be true in all that it affirms. But this does not mean it is always easy to understand. Faith, the indwelling Holy Spirit, and the faith community (the church) serve as aids to help us grasp its truths. This is called the clarity of Scripture. It was meant to be read and understood by God's people. God does not intend to play celestial hide-and-seek with his Word. He desires and delights in revealing himself and his will to us.

Still, there are hard things in the Bible to understand and grasp. For example, why are some stories so graphic? How do we make sense of the evil it portrays? What do we make of events that are seemingly impossible or miraculous? Why would God include talking donkeys, bizarre ways of death, or lead us into a glimpse of the supernatural world that we do not normally see?

No wonder the Bible is the greatest-selling book of all time. Not only is it inspired literature (revealed to us from God), it is full of action, mystery, romance, war, drama, and just about everything else that makes for a good movie. But this is no movie. It is all real. It is our story, our life, our God, and our past, present, and future all wrapped into one.

One thing to explain up front is this: When you step into the worldview of the Bible, you have to understand that the God who made the heavens and the earth is a holy God, and he is dead opposed to anything that violates or offends his holiness and honor. And that's exactly what sin does. When human beings sin, it makes us worthy of judgment—an eternal judgment: "For the wages of sin is death" (Romans 6:23).

God, as a holy God, has the right to execute judgment at any time, at any place, with any method he chooses. So when God called the Israelites to be his instrument of justice by commanding them to destroy the Canaanites who refused to repent of their sin, he was fully justified in carrying out his justice in that manner.

Further, since all of us are born with a sin nature, he doesn't have to let any one of us live. For as the apostle Paul wrote, we are "by nature objects of God's wrath" (Ephesians 2:3). But God is also gracious and loving, slow to anger, and full of mercy. Instead of condemning us instantly, which he has the right to do, he gives common grace to all people and his saving grace to some. In fact, each day we live on this earth and experience all that it gives to us is merely one more act of his abundant grace. The beauty and wonder that surrounds his salvation plan is something we will marvel at for all eternity. His love and mercy are just that great.

So when you read about the various ways and times in which God's judgment and justice fall throughout the pages of the Bible, remember how holy God is and how awful our sin is before him. I fear that many today have lost their reverential fear and understanding of this holy God, and we have accused him of horrific acts of sin when, in fact, it is his fully justified justice.

The Lord is not like us. He is without sin, and when he brings judgment, he is perfectly justified in doing so. As we have said, God is holy. All of his ways are righteous and true. In fact, righteousness and justice are the foundations of his throne (Psalm 89:14).

We do not sit in judgment of God; he sits in judgment of us. We will all give account one day for the things we've done, whether good or bad. The good news is that for the believer in Christ, justice and judgment have already been satisfied by our Savior at the cross. Our God saves, and for whoever believes in him, there is eternal life in him and all the spiritual blessings that God intends for us to enjoy through the power and presence of his indwelling Holy Spirit.

It is my hope that you will enjoy this book. It is designed to be read in short bursts. Each chapter has its own story and its own themes. Feel free to read a chapter or two and put it down, and then come back later to digest more at a different time. In addition to providing brief context to each verse or story and addressing any difficult or perplexing issues that surface, I offer some practical applications and suggestions as to why it is in the Bible.

Truth be told, only God knows why he included everything in the book that he inspired, using at least forty different authors over a period of fifteen hundred years. But we can safely come to conclusions on a great many things as it shares with us the story line that is God's history of salvation for humankind, to be completed in his own sovereign time.

Prepare yourself. Some of this stuff is weird. It's definitely not all rated G. I'm not sure I could even watch if much of this was made into a movie. You may laugh, you may cry. You may scratch your head, and some people in the coffee shop or at home might ask why you are saying, "Ewwwwww, that's gross!" while reading this book. There will likely be things here that you have never read or noticed before. So be prepared, and let's explore these perplexing verses and stories, all the while asking ourselves, *Why is THAT in the Bible?*

1

Abraham and Isaac: The Sacrifice

GENESIS 22:1–14

Why would God ask a man of faith like Abraham to offer up his own son as a sacrifice? Is God sadistic? Had he lost his mind? Was he no different from the false pagan gods (actually demons) of the other nations that required child sacrifices to appease them and keep them happy? These poignant questions enter our minds when we come to the story of Abraham and his son Isaac in Genesis 22. To be fair, our questions are but a human, surface reaction, but they are nonetheless real and deserve answers.

Few people are praised or revered more in Scripture than Abraham. He was the man chosen by God to become the father of a great nation, his name would be made great, and he would be a blessing to the whole earth.

Called to leave his native land and his father's house, Abraham (known as Abram then) set out in faith, not knowing where God was calling him to (Hebrews 11:8). He was to go to a land that would one day be called the Promised Land, a place where he and his children were meant to dwell. Yet Abraham and his wife were barren, so the LORD promised him a son. In fact, he was told his descendants would be as numerous as the stars. To his credit, Abraham believed God.

Abraham became known as a man who was justified by faith (see Genesis 15:6; Romans 4:3, 9, 22; Galatians 3:6; James 2:23), a righteous man, and a "friend of God." He obeyed the LORD by following his commands, and the LORD reconfirmed his covenant with Abraham (symbolized by circumcision and changing his name from Abram to Abraham—meaning "father of many nations").[1] Years would pass before the initial promise was fulfilled, but at the age of one hundred, Abraham and his wife, Sarah (age ninety), finally became parents to Isaac, their firstborn.[2]

One can only imagine their joy. Sarah would finally shed the stigma of being barren, which had huge cultural implications in their day. But even more, God had kept his promise, even though it seemed like there were "years of waiting" that had to be experienced first, years that weren't always handled well.

Prior to Isaac's arrival, in a moment of weakness, Abraham sinfully brought forth a son named Ishmael through Sarah's Egyptian handmaiden Hagar, whom she had urged Abraham to sleep with in a human attempt to speed up the process. But that was not God's plan, and due to the tension in the house between the two women over this child, the maidservant and her son were permanently removed from Abraham's house.[3]

Still, the LORD was gracious to Abraham, and when Isaac finally arrived from Sarah, all was well and right with the world from their perspective. But this is where the story makes a shocking turn. In a profound moment of testing, the LORD commands Abraham to go to Mount Moriah (likely where the modern-day Temple Mount stands) in order to offer up Isaac as a burnt offering and sacrifice.

Why would the LORD ask him to do this? All of Abraham's hopes and dreams were on the line here, as Isaac was supposed to be the child of the promise. Picking up the story line in Genesis 22, try to imagine the shock and terror that would surely accompany anyone who heard this command from the LORD.

> After these things God tested Abraham and said to him, "Abraham!"
> "Here I am," he answered. "Take your son," he said, "your only son
> Isaac, whom you love, go to the land of Moriah, and offer him there
> as a burnt offering on one of the mountains I will tell you about."
>
> Genesis 22:1–2

After Ishmael and his mother, Hagar, were exiled from the family, Isaac became Abraham's "only son," and a loved one at that. He was likely around twenty years old when this command came to Abraham. The amount of faith Abraham had at this point was going to be tested. And that's how the text describes it: a test. Abraham didn't know it was a test, but he knew the LORD. He knew his character. He believed in his promises, and the book of Hebrews tells us later that "he considered God to be able even to raise someone from the dead" (Hebrews 11:19).

Even if Abraham did sacrifice Isaac, which he had every intent to do, he believed God was so faithful to his promises that he would find a way to raise Isaac from the dead.

Honestly, Abraham's faith puts mine to shame. As the father of two boys, I can't imagine being asked to do something like this. But faith sees beyond the present circumstances and trusts in the character of God. Notice there is no hesitation to obey God in the next verses.

> So Abraham got up early in the morning, saddled his donkey, and
> took with him two of his young men and his son Isaac. He split
> wood for a burnt offering and set out to go to the place God had
> told him about. On the third day Abraham looked up and saw the
> place in the distance. Then Abraham said to his young men, "Stay
> here with the donkey. The boy and I will go over there to worship;
> then we'll come back to you."
>
> Genesis 22:3–5

Did you notice the plural form at the end of that last sentence? Abraham did not say, "*I'll* come back to you," but rather, "*we'll* come back to you." Again, Abraham believed God could raise the dead, and apparently he expected it was going to happen right away. Nevertheless, the three-day walk and subsequent walk up the mountain was probably the longest walk of his life, for both Abraham and the confused boy.

> Abraham took the wood for the burnt offering and laid it on his son Isaac. In his hand he took the fire and the knife, and the two of them walked on together. Then Isaac spoke to his father Abraham and said, "My father." And he replied, "Here I am, my son."
> Isaac said, "The fire and the wood are here, but where is the lamb for the burnt offering?" Abraham answered, "God himself will provide the lamb for the burnt offering, my son." Then the two of them walked on together.
>
> Genesis 22:6–8

Remember those words: "*God himself will provide the lamb.*" Those words will have profound meaning, both in the immediate context and in the plan of God's redemption for human history. Apparently, Abraham thought either God would raise his son from the dead, if necessary, or he would provide a lamb as a substitute. Either way, Abraham was not going to stop obeying what surely was a gut-wrenching order.

> When they arrived at the place that God had told him about, Abraham built the altar there and arranged the wood. He bound his son Isaac and placed him on the altar on top of the wood. Then Abraham reached out and took the knife to slaughter his son. But the angel of the Lord called to him from heaven and said, "Abraham, Abraham!" He replied, "Here I am."
> Then he said, "Do not lay a hand on the boy or do anything to him. For now I know that you fear God, since you have not withheld your only son from me." Abraham looked up and saw a ram caught in the thicket by its horns. So Abraham went and took the ram and offered it as a burnt offering in place of his son. And

Abraham named that place The LORD Will Provide, so today it is said: "It will be provided on the LORD's mountain."

Genesis 22:9–14

There are things we wonder about that the story does not tell us. Why would a twenty-year-old let his father bind him on an offering altar? Was there a struggle? Did Isaac believe his father that the LORD would provide a lamb, and is that why he submitted? Did Abraham have to manhandle his son and force him down, or did Isaac offer himself willingly? All these questions fill our minds, but apparently it was not important for us to know the answers. Sometimes Scripture omits details so that we do not get sidetracked and miss the main point.

At the last second, at the height of Abraham's obedience, the LORD steps in to save the day. The LORD affirms Abraham's faith and then provides the lamb. Did Abraham breathe a sigh of relief? I'm sure he did, because what he was about to do would have been completely unnatural to any father. But there's no description of how they felt, only that Abraham saw the LORD's solution when he provided a substitute sacrifice. The question is, Can we see the parallel of the LORD's solution in the person of Jesus?

There is little doubt why this story is in the Bible. Besides being a test for Abraham and a profound example of faith and obedience for us, this story paints a glorious picture that foreshadows the ultimate substitute sacrifice that God himself provided for us. The lamb in the thicket took Isaac's place on the altar of sacrifice, and in the same way, Jesus Christ, God's only Son, took our place on the cross as he willingly offered himself as an atonement for sin. Abraham chose not to hold back his only son, and neither did God.

This story is all about faith, obedience, substitution, and sacrifice—themes recapitulated in the New Testament story of the gospel. Jesus obeyed the Father perfectly, offered himself as a sacrifice in our place (as the "Lamb of God"), and was literally raised from the dead. We, in turn, are called to believe in faith, trust in God's provision of a Lamb to save us from sin, and to validate that faith by living a life of obedience (see James 2:21–23).

I can't think of a better story to illustrate the truth of the gospel. God has provided a lamb. His name is Jesus.

2

Hate Your Family?

≡ LUKE 14:26–27 ≡

When Jesus called the two brothers named Simon [Peter] and Andrew to follow him as disciples, the Bible says that "immediately they left their nets and followed him" (Mark 1:18). The fact is, they had met Jesus before (John 1:35–42), and Andrew previously heard John the Baptist designate Jesus as "the Lamb of God" (John 1:36). So when Jesus found them again along the Sea of Galilee fishing, he called out to them with authority and said, "Follow me, and I will make you fish for people" (Mark 1:17).

Their response was immediate and was designed to be permanent. It came at a cost too, as these men had a lucrative fishing business on the largest freshwater lake in all of Israel. It was a radical lifestyle change, but one that God himself (in human flesh) had called them to embrace wholeheartedly. Little did they know what was in store that would change their lives forever.

Such is the nature of discipleship. Today, for us, it is a radical call to abandon one's previous life of sin, to believe in the life, death, and resurrection of Christ, and to obediently follow his teachings. Though our calling is not to be apostles (as theirs was), Jesus nonetheless calls us as disciples to deny ourselves, to take up our cross daily (figuratively speaking), and to follow him. "For whoever wants to save his life will lose it, but whoever loses his life because of me will save it" (Luke 9:24).

This is God's plan for us: a life of discipleship. All who put their faith and trust in Jesus to save them from sin must also pursue a life that does not live for self, but rather for the glory of God and the priorities of his kingdom. We are to surrender all to Christ, to worship and serve him, and in some cases, even die for him.

In some cultures, the latter is more than just a concept. It is a reality. According to a recent *Christianity Today* article, the two most dangerous countries in which to identify oneself as a Christian are North Korea and Afghanistan.[1] Violence against Christians runs rampant in Pakistan, Nigeria, and the Central African Republic as well. Rape, abuse, imprisonment, social exclusion, and, in many cases, death is the price one may pay for being a follower of Jesus.

Jesus knew this would happen, which is why he said, "If the world hates you, understand that it hated me before it hated you" (John 15:18). So we should expect some hate from the world. Such is the nature of a sinful world system that is demonically inspired to oppose anything that is associated with Christ.

Instead of hate, the essence of the Christian life is *love*. As the apostle Paul rightly told us in 1 Corinthians: "The greatest of these [virtues] is love" (13:13). Now, we can certainly understand the idea that we should "hate" our sin. In fact, James tell us that we should weep and mourn over it (James 4:9), forsaking it as the enemy of a pure and holy life.

There are things that we are not supposed to love, like injustice, violence, and immorality. We are called to love people while standing up for what is right and true, what is pure and God-honoring. Yet if this is all true, why did Jesus make the following statement?

"If anyone comes to me and does not hate his own father and mother, wife and children, brothers and sisters—yes, and even his own life—he cannot be my disciple. Whoever does not bear his own cross and come after me cannot be my disciple."

Luke 14:26–27

Unless my eyes are tricking me, Jesus is telling us we should hate people, and not just anyone, but *our family*. On the surface this makes little sense. It doesn't seem to be consistent with the heart of God or the teaching of the rest of Scripture. So how should we understand it?

Luke 14:26–27 is known as one of the hard sayings of Jesus that need context and clarification. If you cherry-picked this passage out of Scripture, you could walk away with a rather twisted view of things.

In this section of the gospel of Luke, Jesus is teaching something that would not go over well to many modern ears. He is inviting people to be saved by forsaking *anything* that may put up a barrier between them and God, even their very own flesh-and-blood family. There can be, in some instances, quite a cost to discipleship. In certain Muslim countries, a person who converts to Christianity may be banned from their family, imprisoned, tortured, or, in some extreme cases, murdered, all for choosing Christ.

As New Testament scholar Darrell Bock writes, "Discipleship is fundamentally a call to allegiance. Jesus is to have first place over all, including family."[2] Jesus is to be our first love (Revelation 2:4), and if that means our families abandon us or their priorities are in direct conflict to our pursuit of following Christ, we must choose Christ over family. "Other concerns are to take second place to following Jesus."[3]

This idea is a reality for many Christians, even in America. Some believers have felt the scrutiny, criticism, or ostracism that comes within a family that does not regard or prioritize Christ or his will as a priority in life. In a self-focused "me" culture, where religious commitment is often demonized or relegated to "extremism," following Christ and embracing a life of discipleship that includes moral boundaries may seem foolish. And the repercussions for that choice may feel like one is bearing "his own cross," as Jesus explicitly states in verse 27 above.

But the question is, Why did Jesus use the word *hate* in the passage above? We can certainly understand that an unbelieving family may marginalize us if we follow Jesus, but do we have to "hate" them in return? Certainly not, at least not in the way we commonly think.

This is where we need to understand the first-century Jewish context this statement was delivered in. The idea of "hate" was not to be taken literally. It was used as a rhetorical device that communicated the idea of "loving something less" in a comparative sense. Pastor John MacArthur explains this well.

> The Lord's teaching that it is necessary to *hate* one's family is not inconsistent with the Bible's commands that children are to honor their parents (Exodus 20:12), husbands love their wives (Ephesians 5:25), wives love their husbands (Titus 2:4), and parents love their children (Titus 2:4; cf. Ephesians 6:4). *Hate in this context is a Semitic way of expressing preference.* For example, God said in Malachi 1:2–3, "I have loved Jacob; but I have hated Esau" (cf. Romans 9:13). The point is not that God had animosity toward Esau, but rather he preferred Jacob by giving his promise through him . . . to hate one's family is to prefer God over them by disregarding what they desire if that conflicts with what God requires; it is to love God more and them less.[4]

This is why surface readings of Bible verses without understanding the culture, context, and communicative methods of that day can be misleading at times. We need to keep several things in mind. Deeper study is required whenever we come across something like this that seems to shock our first impressions. Second, the Bible never contradicts itself. So if a dilemma like this surfaces, we must trust that there is a better explanation that can be reconciled with whatever Scripture teaches elsewhere.

Third, many idioms and sayings and comparative rhetorical devices common in that day need explanation if they are to be understood over two thousand years later. This is not to say that the Bible does not have clarity or is impossible to understand, but rather, certain sections require us to mentally time-travel back to a time and place that is different from ours so that we can understand the original author's intent.

The word *hate* in the context in which Jesus delivered it meant something very different from all the ideas we import into that word today. Nevertheless, it still presented a challenge to anyone who would have to "count the cost" of following Christ.

This was all designed to weed out superficial followers of Christ. To be sure, there were many. By the time Jesus said this during his ministry, his popularity was strong even though he was despised by the religious elite of Israel who were nothing but hypocrites and frauds. But Jesus knew that not all who professed to believe in him and follow him were sincere.

Some came just to hear this amazing man speak. Others were drawn to his miracles, his ability to provide food (feeding of thousands), cast out demons, heal the sick, raise the dead, etc. And within that number there were those who truly believed and those who did not. So to sort out the half-hearted from the true disciples, Jesus made the cost of discipleship exceptionally high. Bock helps us conclude this chapter with a helpful summary:

> At that time a Jewish person who made a choice for Jesus would alienate his own family. If someone desired acceptance by family more than a relationship with God, one might never come to Jesus, given the rejection that would inevitably follow. In other words, there could be no casual devotion to Jesus in the first century. A decision for Christ marked a person and automatically came at a cost.[5]

So for us, what is the cost of following Jesus? Will it mean we will be labeled as social outcasts? Will it cost us certain relationships, our jobs, our reputation, finances? Will it mean being labeled as "haters" because we do not embrace the new sexual orthodoxy that is prevailing in secular culture today? There may be a cost to embracing moral boundaries and all that is associated with the name and teachings of Christ and God's Word.

The good news is, for those who follow the narrow path that leads to eternal life, the eternal rewards far outweigh any temporary pains and griefs we might have to endure today. For as Jesus said,

> "Whoever wants to save his life will lose it, but whoever loses his life because of me will save it."
>
> Luke 9:24

3

An Annoyed Apostle Takes Action

In a recent episode of the hit television show *Family Feud*, contestants were asked to name a creature they wished would go extinct sooner than later. No one could give an answer that scored many points, but they all nodded when the number one answer was revealed: the mosquito. Though it is an important part of the food chain, no one particularly likes a flying insect that has a crazy buzzing sound and stealthily seeks to suck your blood while causing your skin to swell up and itch. We might all feel we could have done quite well without that aspect of creation.

To be fair, many things in this world have the propensity to irritate us, whether it be traffic, certain alarm sounds, or even people.

One peculiar instance of annoyance in the Bible comes from the book of Acts, where the apostle Paul and his entourage were on one of his missionary journeys and being followed by a "slave girl" who was possessed by an evil spirit of divination. The girl was essentially a fortune-teller, a medium who was in contact with demonic spirits in an attempt to predict the future, a practice clearly condemned in the Law of Moses (Deuteronomy 18:9–12). Moreover, the Bible is clear that only God knows the future and what it holds (Isaiah 46:9–10). God is the only omniscient being who can step outside of time and see it all at once.

Apparently, the demons within her were interested in harassing the apostle and his team because of their spreading of the gospel. Perhaps the demons were even interested in confusing Paul's audience, which I will explain in a minute. But first, the account from Dr. Luke in Acts 16.

> Once, as we were on our way to prayer, a slave girl met us who had a spirit by which she predicted the future. She made a large profit for her owners by fortune-telling. As she followed Paul and us she cried out, "These men, who are proclaiming to you the way of salvation, are the servants of the Most High God." She did this for many days. Paul was greatly annoyed. . . .
>
> Acts 16:16–18

On the surface, most people wouldn't see this as too problematic. Everything she said was true in one sense, at least one might think so. In Romans 1:1 Paul called himself a "slave" (Holman Christian Standard Bible) or "bond-servant" (NASB) of Christ, and he and the others were certainly proclaiming the "way of salvation" through the gospel of Christ. So, what's the problem?

For starters, the source of the information was an issue. Paul did not want someone filled with demons to be testifying to their identity and mission. Even Jesus did not want a demon to testify to his identity in Luke 4:34 because he did not want the truth about him to be connected to the demonic. There is no reason to affirm the testimony of demons to the point that people start believing what they say, horrible creatures that they are, even if what they say is true.

Paul did not want the slave girl who often spoke for many "false gods" to be speaking on their behalf, because it could potentially mislead people into thinking that this girl was a legitimate spokesperson whenever she spoke. Further, she used the phrase, "servants of the Most High God." And even though that phrase is used of Yahweh, the one true God, nearly fifty times in the Old Testament, in the context of the pagan city of Philippi, the title "Most High God" had a very different connotation. New Testament scholar Darrell Bock explains:

> They serve the "Most High God," a key description of God in a polytheistic environment but one that could be misunderstood because *non-Jewish religions also used the expression for pagan gods* . . . in other words, she could have been understood as saying that Paul's God was the highest among many gods, because the expression is not necessarily a reference to Yahweh but simply to a supreme god of one's preference.[1]

If she would have been primarily in a Jewish audience, the phrase would have struck a true chord with the listeners, but since she was in a pagan audience, where the title meant something very different, it was not helpful for her to be shouting something that could mislead the audience, who would hear it with its pagan connotations.

The girl kept following Paul and his team around for many days, shouting this out to all who would listen. Paul tolerated it at first, but apparently Paul eventually became seriously annoyed by it (literally "deeply disturbed, burdened, worked up, or irritated"). He decided to do something about it in order to show the power and authority of Jesus' name above all other so-called gods.

> She did this for many days. Paul was greatly annoyed. Turning to the spirit, he said, "I command you in the name of Jesus Christ to come out of her!" And it came out right away.

Paul exercised his apostolic authority and cast the demon out of the girl.[2] The demon had no choice but to obey, and she was immediately delivered. The fact that Paul mentions *Jesus' name* makes it clear that the "Most High God" referred to earlier need not be confused with any of the pagan gods. Paul is not speaking for them, but rather he is speaking on behalf of the *one true God* of the universe, the man Christ Jesus, the Yahweh of the Old Testament.

Just then, everything changed. The "supernatural" within the girl that made her masters so much money was now missing, and they countered by seizing Paul and Silas and dragged them into the public circle to falsely accuse them of "public insurrection and disturbances" before the authorities. They even made sure to call Paul and Silas "Jews" in order to drum up even more emotion by appealing to the anti-Semitism of the Roman culture common in that day. They said, "[They] are promoting customs that are not legal for us as Romans to adopt or practice" (Acts 16:21).

The crowd responds with rage, and the magistrates order that Paul and Silas be stripped and beaten with rods, only later to be thrown in prison with their feet put in stocks (vv. 23–24). The mob mentality prevailed, and the irony is that now the girl who once was treated as a slave is now spiritually free, and Paul and Silas who were spiritually free are now put in physical bondage, treated like slaves.

It won't be long until Paul and Silas (who end up singing hymns of praise even while wounded and bound) are delivered from their human bondage, thanks to an earthquake.

But what can we take from the story of an annoyed apostle and a spiritually trafficked slave girl who is possessed by a demon and won't shut up? Simply this: Satan may seek to destroy the church and the spread of the gospel any way he can, but he will not prevail (see Matthew 16:18). His ways are often subtle, and even in this story, the girl's testimony may have fooled people into thinking she was part of Paul's entourage and was a reliable source of truth, but she was not.

This is how many false teachers work today, using biblical terms without biblical definitions, giving a little hint of truth, and using their "credibility" to ultimately lead others astray. Let us be clear, however; those kinds of people are empowered by Satan.

This story serves as a warning about Satan's schemes. At the same time, it highlights this wonderful truth: The gospel of Jesus Christ has the power to change lives and deliver people from bondage while testifying to the *one true God* who has supremacy and authority over all things. It is only in the name of Christ that one can be delivered from that which enslaves. And we see that truth front and center in this story.

Even so, Paul and Silas experienced the hatred that naturally comes from the world, which often values money and material things over spiritual truth. But it couldn't take away their joy. Even bruised and bleeding and bound, they sang God's praises. There is an intimacy and joy found in the "fellowship of sharing in [Christ's] sufferings" (Philippians 3:10), and it is in those moments that God's love and presence are sweeter than anything else in life that may temporarily annoy us.

4

Balaam and the Talking Donkey

=== NUMBERS 22 ===

A talking donkey? Really?! In what sounds a lot like the movie *Shrek* (with a talking and quite humorous donkey), the Bible has its own "animated animal" who apparently was temporarily granted the ability to communicate with its owner. Indeed, the God of the universe, who created the world from nothing, also has the power to make a donkey talk.

This is yet another Old Testament miracle. The story revolves around a pagan false prophet by the name of Balaam, a Moabite king named Balak, and a fast approaching group of Israelites led by Moses who were making their way toward the Promised Land, conquering the people and the lands the LORD commanded them to take.

When Balak, the Moabite king, saw the Israelites approaching and camping in the plains of Moab, he panicked and reached out to another people group, the Midianites. He conjured up a plan to use the services of the false prophet Balaam, an evil man whose reputation was one of putting both blessings and curses on people. Thinking that Balaam could be called upon and paid to curse

Israel, the king of Moab sent messengers from the two people groups to the false prophet with the "fees for divination" in hand.

It is then that the God of Israel intervenes and speaks to the pagan prophet, warning him not to go with the messengers and not to curse God's people because of the fact that they are already blessed. Though it is clear that Balaam hears the LORD, it is also obvious that the prophet does not know or have a saving relationship with Israel's God.[1] To him, the LORD is just another one of the so-called gods of individual nations. But he is not about to get on the bad side of any "god." So when the messengers come for Balaam, he refuses to go, just like God instructed him.

But the Moabite king decides to follow up yet again and sends an even greater entourage of leaders who come bearing more impressive promises in order to lure and bribe the false prophet to come to their aid. God then speaks to Balaam a second time, and permits him to go *on the condition that he only says and does what God commands*. But when Balaam arises to go the next day, God decides to send the "angel of the LORD" to stand in his way. Apparently, God knew that Balaam was more interested in the money than in obeying God (see v. 32), so God sent the angel of the LORD to be Balaam's adversary (Numbers 22:22), resulting in one of the most entertaining moments of the Old Testament.

> Balaam was riding his donkey, and his two servants were with him. When the donkey saw the angel of the LORD standing on the path with a drawn sword in his hand, she turned off the path and went into the field. So Balaam hit her to return her to the path. Then the angel of the LORD stood in a narrow passage between the vineyards, with a stone wall on either side. The donkey saw the angel of the LORD and pressed herself against the wall, squeezing Balaam's foot against it. So he hit her once again. The angel of the LORD went ahead and stood in a narrow place where there was no room to turn to the right or the left. When the donkey saw the angel of the LORD, she crouched down under Balaam. So he became furious and beat the donkey with his stick.
>
> Numbers 22:22–27

I can just see this donkey doing what donkeys do, all saddled up with Balaam perched on top, trotting down the path, only to look up to see a glorious angel standing in the way with a sword in his hand. And the donkey's thinking, *Nope, not going THAT way*.[2] But every time she veers off the path or tries to avoid the angel, she gets whacked by Balaam and eventually she just lies down.[3]

So now we are at an impasse. The donkey sees into the spiritual realm, but Balaam cannot. Perhaps God is contrasting the unbelieving pagan seer *who cannot see* with one of God's own creatures who *can see*.[4] In this way, unbelief seemingly makes man dumber than a donkey. Nevertheless, the donkey is going nowhere, and neither is an angry Balaam. But God decides to step in and the unimaginable happens.

> Then the LORD opened the donkey's mouth, and she asked Balaam, "What have I done to you that you have beaten me these three times?" Balaam answered the donkey, "You made me look like a fool. If I had a sword in my hand, I'd kill you now!" But the donkey said, "Am I not the donkey you've ridden all your life until today? Have I ever treated you this way before?" "No," he replied.
>
> Numbers 22:28–30

I don't know what's more incredulous, that the donkey spoke in a human language or that Balaam thought it was feasible to answer her back. Both seem to be out of the ordinary, but as Timothy Ashley points out, "To discuss whether donkeys have sufficient vocal cords to speak overlooks the fact that this is an act of Almighty Yahweh. The question of how the donkey could speak does not concern the narrator [of the story]."[5]

Meanwhile, as Balaam gets *hysterical*, the donkey gets *historical*. She asks her master whether she has ever behaved like this in the past, and Balaam is forced to answer with a simple "no." The obvious notion is that Balaam should know that something else has to be going on here. But without eyes to see the angel or the LORD's bigger purpose (both here and with Israel as a whole), Balaam is blind and handicapped. Then yet another miracle takes place.

Then the LORD opened Balaam's eyes, and he saw the angel of the LORD standing in the path with a drawn sword in his hand. Balaam knelt low and bowed in worship on his face. The angel of the LORD asked him, "Why have you beaten your donkey these three times? Look, I came out to oppose you, because I consider what you are doing to be evil. The donkey saw me and turned away from me these three times. If she had not turned away from me, I would have killed you by now and let her live."

Numbers 22:31–33

God opened the donkey's mouth, and now he has opened Balaam's eyes. The donkey has been vindicated while Balaam is humiliated. The apostle Peter would later write, "For a mute donkey, speaking with the voice of a man, restrained the madness of the prophet" (2 Peter 2:16 NASB). The fact is, the donkey saved Balaam's life, for the angel would have certainly killed Balaam because of his evil intent. Balaam, then, in the next verses confesses his sin and ignorance, and offers to return home.

Instead, the angel instructs him to go forward anyway, but he is not to curse or collect anything from the king. He is only to obey the will of God and to say what God tells him to say. So Balaam goes, and in the same way he opened the donkey's mouth, the LORD put words in Balaam's mouth, speaking no fewer than three oracles of blessing (not cursing) on God's people, the Israelites.

But this is not what the king had in mind, and now the king is furious and feels duped. So he and Balaam part ways, and no payment or honor will be given to the prophet. Meanwhile, we can only hope that Balaam will walk away irrevocably changed by his encounter with the true and living God, but this is not the case. For later in the book, Balaam is credited with helping to entice the Israelites into sexual sin and idolatry with the daughters of Moab (Numbers 31:16).

He is not a good man, and even though he at one point confessed his sin (22:34), he did not fully repent and believe in the LORD. In fact, he was later identified as the pagan "diviner" (someone who sought knowledge from demons) who ended up being killed by the Israelites (Joshua 13:22). The apostle Peter would call him a man who "loved the ways of unrighteousness" (2 Peter 2:15), just like the false teachers of his day.

Even worse, the Lord Jesus Christ in the book of Revelation said that Balaam was one who "taught Balak [the Moabite king] to place a stumbling block in front of the Israelites: to eat meat sacrificed to idols and to commit sexual immorality" (Revelation 2:14).

So what do we learn from this story? Many things. First, God's will and God's plans will prevail, no matter how much Satan seeks to corrupt and destroy them. Here in this story, God would not allow his people to be cursed. He had plans to bring at least a remnant into the Promised Land. And even today, in his church, God's will shall still come to pass even though there are attacks from without and false teachers from within. This is to God's glory that he will always lead us in triumphal procession in Christ (2 Corinthians 2:14). Let us always remember that he took the curse (on the cross) so that we get the blessing.

Further, Balaam's story teaches us that not all who claim to speak for God belong to God. Balaam was known as a seer or prophet, but he was thoroughly corrupt, a prophet for sale. In fact, he was a consultant to many demons. He did not truly believe in the LORD with saving faith, and he only spoke God's words because he was compelled by God to speak it—otherwise, he was in it for money and fame. This describes many false teachers of our day as well. Some speak a hint of truth, but their motives are corrupt, and their true lives will one day be revealed and they will be judged just like Balaam.

Finally, God is yet again a God of miracles. Yes, a donkey speaks just like the serpent who spoke in the garden of Eden. These are not normal occurrences, but they are not impossible, because we have a God who is able to do immeasurably more than all we ask or imagine (Ephesians 3:20). Stories like this remind us that our sovereign and all-powerful God is always and ultimately in control. We may even need a talking donkey to remind us of who is in charge and directs our paths.

5

"Emasculate Themselves!"

GALATIANS 5:12

I have often wondered about the personalities of the apostles. What was Peter like? Was he strong, down to earth, and clever with lots of funny stories as many fishermen are? Or how about James, the Lord's half brother? As the leader in the church in Jerusalem, he had a reputation of being strong in the faith, articulate, and practical, with a godliness (he was called James the Just) that even unbelievers took notice of.

Surely one of the more interesting apostles we will get to spend time with in heaven is Paul. What a brilliant thinker, full of passion for God's truth, eager to please Christ, and willing to suffer greatly for the gospel. Paul was trained by the best of the best in his pre-conversion days, educated by Gamaliel, the leading Pharisee of his day "held in high honor by all the people" (Acts 5:34 ESV).

As an expert in the Mosaic law, Paul was one of the most well-educated and talented young lawyers of his day when he was called by Christ to faith. He knew God's Word inside and out, following the regulations of the Old Testament law such that he could call himself "blameless" or "faultless" (Philippians 3:6).[1] But none of that "old life" before Christ had any spiritual value or merit now that Paul had come to saving faith in Jesus.

In fact, though he had a foundation in the Old Testament Scriptures, Paul now recognized all those attempts of a self-righteous, self-justifying, legalistic lifestyle as mere "dung" compared to the righteousness that was credited to him and his account when Christ found him and saved him (Philippians 3:8). To exchange his human attempts at righteousness for the perfect and imputed righteousness of Christ that came to him by faith was a no-brainer.

Paul[2] never wanted to go back to the old way of life with all of its constant struggle and striving to maintain Mosaic law. Attempting to maintain the law out of the human flesh to gain some kind of favor or salvation was exhausting. First off, it was impossible to do, and it was not the law's intent anyway. The law was designed to teach us about God's holiness and standards, our inability to keep it perfectly, and to show us how much we needed a Savior to rescue us from its condemnation. In short, the law was designed to point us to our need for Christ so that we might be justified by faith in him (Galatians 3:19, 24).

The good news about Jesus delivered Paul from his ignorant zeal, his pride and sinful self-righteousness, and his unending and tiring effort to try to justify himself before God with his works.

So when false teachers infiltrated the church in Galatia and began advocating that anyone who wanted to be a "good Christian" had to also follow the Law of Moses and be circumcised, Paul about popped a vein in his head.

> You foolish Galatians! Who has cast a spell on you, before whose eyes Jesus Christ was publicly portrayed as crucified? I only want to learn this from you: Did you receive the Spirit by the works of the law or by believing what you heard? Are you so foolish? After beginning by the Spirit, are you now finishing by the flesh?
>
> Galatians 3:1–3

Paul was livid. He couldn't believe the church was falling for the lies and tricks of the false teachers (called "Judaizers"), who were saying it was necessary to adopt Jewish laws and customs to be truly saved and a part of the "people of God."[3] To go back to following the "works of the law" was an affront to the gospel of Christ, which clearly teaches we are saved by grace through faith alone in the life, death, and resurrection of Jesus Christ.

Righteousness is not to be achieved by any human "doings" of any kind, but rather is based on what Christ has done for us on our behalf. In Paul's words,

> Know that a person is not justified by the works of the law, but by faith in Jesus Christ. So we, too, have put our faith in Christ Jesus that we may be justified by faith in Christ and not by the works of the law, because by the works of the law no one will be justified.
>
> Galatians 2:16

Much like Jesus, Paul reserved some of his strongest words for the false teachers who purported to be righteous but were actually leading people away from the blessings and benefits of grace (Galatians 5:4). The ones who were advocating that they must be circumcised like a Jew in order to be counted as righteous were actually enemies of the cross, inviting the Galatians back into what Paul called a "yoke of slavery" (Galatians 5:1). All they were doing was seeking to alienate people from the benefits that Christ purchased for them.

It is here that we see both a righteous anger and a profoundly sarcastic rant that stemmed from the personality of the apostle Paul. The words speak for themselves.

> You were running well. Who hindered you from obeying the truth? . . . the one who is troubling you will bear the penalty, whoever he is. . . . I wish those who unsettle you would emasculate themselves!
>
> Galatians 5:7, 10, 12

Paul held nothing back here. In fact, some think Paul was being inappropriate. Why would he suggest that these false teachers practice self-mutilation? The word that Paul uses in the Greek is *apokoptō*, which means "to cut off." What Paul seems to be saying is that those who are advocating circumcision should just go the whole way and fully castrate themselves.

I don't think Paul was merely using figurative language either, as some have suggested, though it is certainly true he would have wanted these false teachers to be "cut off" from the body of Christ in a spiritual and literal sense (as in, leave the church altogether). Rather, I think Paul seriously wanted to see if these false teachers were bold enough to proclaim a spiritual devotion akin to what a eunuch would practice.

In Bible times, eunuchs were male servants who often served in royal households and were purposefully castrated so as to protect the king's wives and concubines from bringing forth children by them (see, for example, 2 Kings 9:32). People also became eunuchs out of some misguided devotion to their religion in order to show that their passions were not for sexual things but rather for their god. This was twisted thinking. Even the Law of Moses excluded eunuchs from the temple: "No one who has been emasculated by crushing or cutting may enter the assembly of the Lord" (Deuteronomy 23:1 NIV).

Still, at the time Paul wrote this, pagan priests from a cult known as Cybele would physically mutilate themselves as part of their rituals.

As theologian Philip Ryken writes, "So perhaps Paul was saying something like this: 'Look, if you insist on getting circumcised, you are trying to be saved by a ritual. But that is just another form of paganism, so you might as well go the whole way and become one of their priests!'"[4]

Believe me, if any so-called god required something that extreme as an expression of religious devotion, that god is not worth following. Nope, not going to do it. No way.

Paul likely knew that the false teachers, who loved themselves so much, would likely never go that far, but hopefully they would cut themselves off in one sense by leaving the church altogether. You can truly hear the righteous anger in Paul's tone, and because his words were inspired by the Holy Spirit, we can also get a sense of how God himself felt about these false teachers and how he used Paul's personality and rhetorical force to get the point across.

The biblical writers were not puppets. Though God inspired what they penned, they did not practice divine dictation where they had no personality or experiences of their own involved in writing the text. Surely what they wrote down came from God and was perfect, but it was not devoid of human instrumentation, though we must also make it clear that it is the text itself and not the writer who is perfect. As Peter rightly said,

> No prophecy ever came by the will of man; instead, men spoke from God as they were carried along by the Holy Spirit.
>
> 2 Peter 1:21

Why is this graphic text in the Bible then? For me, it is clear. It is here to show how heinous it is to lead others away from the gospel of grace through false teaching. It is here for the Galatians to hear how serious and zealous they must be to guard themselves from the fleshly temptation to revert back to performance-based salvation. For that line of thinking is an affront to the cross, nullifies the purpose of our Savior's coming, and puts us back on a frustrating path that would only lead one to hell. It does not and will not ever justify someone before God. Not by works, lest anyone should boast (Ephesians 2:9).

6

Justification by Faith Alone?

W hat do we do when we see an apparent contradiction in the Bible? For example, some have pointed out that in the healing of a blind man named Bartimaeus in the gospel accounts, Matthew and Mark say that Jesus was "leaving Jericho" (Matthew 20:29–30; Mark 10:46), but Luke says that he was "coming to" or "approaching" Jericho when this story took place (Luke 18:35).

In addition, Matthew says there were "two blind men sitting by the roadside" (Matthew 20:30), but both Mark and Luke record only *one* blind man sitting by the roadside, who shouted out to Jesus, "Jesus, Son of David, have mercy on me!" (Mark 10:46–47; Luke 18:35–38).

These accounts seem to be saying something contradictory. Which is it? Was he *coming* or *going*, and was there *one* or *two* blind men? This is a perfect example of where further digging and research as well as the process known as *harmonization* may be of help.

First, concerning the city of Jericho, there was an old city of Jericho (in ruins) and a new city of Jericho that was built nearby. So Jesus could have been moving from the old city to the new city or vice versa, and in that case he would have been either coming or going, depending on which city the gospel writers were using as their reference point.

Second, with respect to the blind men, the gospel writers have simply chosen to highlight different details of the account—but where there are two blind men, it is also true that there is also at least one. This is simply called "harmonization," and it is not a contradiction. When all the details are merged together, it still makes sense.

Another example of an apparent contradiction (this time a *theological* contradiction instead of a factual one) is what Paul says about how a person is justified before God versus what James says about justification. First, what Paul says:

> For no one will be justified in his sight by works of the law. . . . (Romans 3:20).

> They are justified freely by his grace through the redemption that is in Christ Jesus (Romans 3:24).

> For we conclude that a person is justified by faith apart from the works of the law (Romans 3:28).

> By the works of the law no human being will be justified (Galatians 2:16).

I think we can get the picture. To be justified is to be made right before God, and it includes both the idea of a legal exoneration from sin via forgiveness as well as a declaration of being made righteous in God's sight (in terms of spiritual standing) due to the righteousness of Christ that is credited to us. And Paul insists that all of this comes to us by *faith alone* and not by any works. His classic and climactic expression of this is in Ephesians 2.

> For you are saved by grace through faith, and this is not from your-
> selves; it is God's gift—not from works, so that no one can boast.
>
> Ephesians 2:8–9

Thus, Paul makes it abundantly clear that there is nothing that we can do to *earn* our salvation. We are not justified before God by the things that we do, whether it is following the Old Testament laws or any other types of works. Rather, we are made right by simply placing saving faith in Jesus Christ, whose perfect life, sacrificial and atoning death, and subsequent resurrection are the basis of any believer's acceptance before God.[1]

This was one of the main themes of the Protestant Reformation when the doctrine of justification was "rediscovered" or reemphasized by the likes of Martin Luther and others who argued that we were saved *sola fide* ("by faith alone") in the gospel or "good news" about Jesus Christ.

But then if this is true (and I am arguing that it is), what do we do with what James says in James 2 when he seemingly says the exact opposite?

> What good is it, my brothers and sisters, if someone claims to have faith but does not have works? Can such faith save him? . . .
>
> Senseless person! Are you willing to learn that faith without works is useless? Wasn't Abraham our father justified by works in offering Isaac his son on the altar? You see that faith was active together with his works, and by works, faith was made complete, and the Scripture was fulfilled that says, Abraham believed God, and it was credited to him as righteousness, and he was called God's friend. *You see that a person is justified by works and not by faith alone.* In the same way, wasn't Rahab the prostitute also justified by works in receiving the messengers and sending them out by a different route? For just as the body without the spirit is dead, so also faith without works is dead.
>
> James 2:14, 20–26, emphasis mine

James seems to be saying something quite different from Paul. He is linking the importance of works to the idea of justification, using Abraham as an example. In fact, he says very clearly that "a person is justified by works and *not by faith alone*." That doesn't seem to jive with what Paul said in the aforementioned verses. In fact, this is why Martin Luther had an unfavorable view of the book of James, calling it an "epistle of straw."

How can we reconcile this seemingly apparent theological contradiction? The answer is understanding that Paul and James are coming at the idea of justification from two different angles. Paul is talking about the very foundation and basis of our justification, and James is talking about how justification, if it is true that we have it, will always result in evidence of its authenticity by the fruit it produces, namely good works.

The Greek word for *justification* can have two meanings or senses. The first sense has to do with acquittal or declaring someone righteous (Paul's use above), and the second sense is *vindication or proof of righteousness* (James's use here). James's argument is different from Paul's because he is trying to convince us that "faith without works" is really not saving faith at all. In fact, it is dead and useless (James 2:17, 20).

Notice that James reaffirms what Paul also taught when he quoted Genesis 15:6 above in verse 23, saying that "Abraham believed God, and it was credited to him as righteousness." In other words, Abraham was saved by faith alone—but James goes on to emphasize it is a faith that is never without works (lest it be a dead faith). Rather, the heart of true saving faith will always demonstrate its credibility and be vindicated by producing genuine spiritual fruit.

James tells us how Abraham's saving faith was proven to be real by his obedience to God in offering up his son Isaac on the altar (see chapter 1 of this book), and by showing us that Rahab the prostitute's saving faith in the Old Testament was verified, proven, and authenticated by her actions concerning the spies that she hid and redirected away from danger in the midst of Israel's conquest of Jericho in Joshua 2.

Putting all this together—we are saved by grace through faith alone (Ephesians 2:8), but true saving faith will always produce works; it must always be "accompanied by action" (James 2:17). Otherwise, it is nothing but dead, useless faith—or no faith at all.

Understanding the context and the angle of both Paul's and James's arguments helps to harmonize the Scriptures so that we have a complete and accurate picture of what the Bible teaches. The Bible does not contradict itself. There is an amazing internal consistency both factually and theologically throughout its pages. The reason this is true is because we as Christians believe that the Holy Spirit is the one who inspired all of Scripture, from Genesis to Revelation.

Though he used the personalities and contexts of each writer who wrote down what God intended for us (see 2 Peter 1:21), the Spirit is nevertheless the divine author behind the texts, which are "God-breathed" (2 Timothy 3:16) or inspired. As such, the truthfulness and inerrancy of Scripture is rooted in the character of God himself, who does not lie. Jesus himself said in his prayer to the Father that "your word is truth" (John 17:17).

Because these texts originate from the heart of God, we can rest assured that they are fully inspired, without error in the original manuscripts, internally consistent, factually true (when all the facts are known), and non-contradictory.

During the season of the Protestant Reformation, the reformers taught an interpretive principle known as *the analogy of faith*. This idea is that the Scriptures are the work of one divine mind, and as such are reliable and self-consistent without any contradiction. This means that the Scriptures do not contradict themselves, and that if there is difficulty in understanding what is being taught, we must let Scripture help us interpret Scripture.[2]

In other words, some places in Scripture speak very clearly to us with great clarity. And if we know that we've understood it correctly in one place, we must let that understanding guide us in our interpretations of Scripture elsewhere, especially the more difficult sections. We just used this principle above when we let a clear understanding of what Paul taught about justification by faith help us understand the altogether different emphasis of James who was coming at it from a very different angle.

So Paul and James are not up there in heaven duking it out. They have always been in agreement with each other. We must be careful to understand the background, context, and audience of the writers, for it is only in gathering all the facts that we can have a clearer assessment of what God intends for us to know and understand concerning his "word of truth."

7

"Lead Us Not into Temptation"

$$\equiv \text{MATTHEW } 6:13 \equiv$$

One of the most beloved prayers in all the Bible is the Lord's Prayer in the Sermon on the Mount in Matthew 6. Jesus presented the prayer as a model for his disciples, a prayer they were to embrace and use in their own lives. So rather than being the Lord's Prayer (as if Jesus were praying it), it might be better referred to as the "Disciples' Prayer," since Jesus was teaching his followers how to pray.

Because Jesus was using it as an example, it serves as a guide, not merely a liturgy (even though it can and has been used that way). It is brief, simple, and comprehensive. It does not cover everything we should or could pray for, but it gets to the heart of our relationship with God and others. Of the six petitions or requests, three are aimed at God and three are directed toward our human needs.

The prayer begins by recognizing God's sovereignty over all things as the God who is in heaven, along with a recognition that God's name and all that it stands for is "hallowed" (or regarded as holy). Then we are invited to pray for the kingdom of God "to

44

come," that more people would come to know and love Christ as their Lord and Savior and that his reign and rule in our lives would become increasingly prevalent as we submit to him.

Further, as we pray for his kingdom to come, we ultimately desire his second coming to earth, whereby his kingdom will be fully revealed in a spiritual, physical, and political sense in his future reign upon the earth (Revelation 22:20).

Next we are invited to pray for our "daily bread," which certainly includes food and even more, all that we need to sustain us in life. Perhaps our greatest need that Jesus meets is our need for forgiveness, and as we pray for that, we are also reminded to be a forgiving person.

But then we are led to pray about something that has troubled many people. The prayer continues, "and lead us not into temptation, but deliver us from evil" (Matthew 6:13 ESV).[1]

Not many have taken issue with the request to "deliver us from evil," but the first phrase of verse 13 has caused a great deal of controversy. We are asking God *not* to lead us into temptation. The problem with that on the surface is this: Why would God *ever* lead us into temptation? That is something that the Bible says God would *never* do. For James 1:13–15 tells us,

> When tempted, no one should say, "God is tempting me." For God cannot be tempted by evil, nor does he tempt anyone; but each one is tempted when, by his own evil desire, he is dragged away and enticed. Then, after desire has conceived, it gives birth to sin; and sin, when it is full-grown, gives birth to death.
>
> James 1:13–15 NIV 1984

In June 2019, Pope Francis of the Roman Catholic Church authorized a change to the Catholic Bible's translation of the passage in the Italian liturgy. He changed it from "lead us not into temptation" to "do not let us fall into temptation," because he suggested that the former translation communicates the idea that God induces temptation. But further study and reflection is essential here in order to understand that this is not what the Lord's Prayer is suggesting. Even more problematic is the fact that the pope is essentially changing what Jesus said.

So what did he mean then? What are we praying for here? If we are asking God not to lead us into temptation, but that's something he would never do in the first place, there has to be a slightly different understanding of what we are asking him for.

The key may rest in the original translation of *temptation*. The Greek word may also mean "testing." But how might this solve the problem, since the Holy Spirit led Jesus himself into a time of "testing" in Luke 4 when Jesus was in the wilderness with the devil. Further, the idea of testing is found in the Old Testament as well, when Moses said to Israel,

> Remember that the LORD your God led you on the entire journey these forty years in the wilderness, so that he might humble you and test you to know what was in your heart, whether or not you would keep his commands.
>
> Deuteronomy 8:2

God may purposefully put us into a time of testing in order to humble, transform, and strengthen us, wean us off the flesh so that we rely on him, or even prepare us for greater challenges we may face that may require our complete obedience to him.

If putting us *to the test* is another viable translation of that word, then why would Jesus tell us to pray for that not to happen?

This is where the second half of the petition actually adds light to the gray area. Coupled with this petition is the idea of being "delivered" from evil, or the Evil One (the devil himself). In this case, it helps us understand that our prayer *not to be led into temptation or testing* is a prayer to protect us from our propensity to sin whenever we find ourselves in such moments.

New Testament scholar David Pao remarks,

> The petition likely assumes the presence (and the coming) of periods of testing, and this petition should then be understood as a call to

God for protecting His people from falling into sin in the midst of such testing (Matthew 26:39, 41).[2]

We want to be spared from a "trial or temptation that results in a fall."[3] We are asking God to deliver us from those kinds of challenges. Pastor-teacher John Piper properly summarizes the "lead us not into temptation" petition in his paraphrasing prayer:

Father, since "a man's steps are from the Lord" (Proverbs 20:24), forbid, we pray, that any temptation we encounter by your leading would trap us and suck us in with no way of escape. For you are faithful, and you have promised that with every temptation "you will provide the way of escape, that we may be able to endure it" (1 Corinthians 10:13).

Do for us, dear Father, what you did for Jesus, when you "*led* (!) him by the Spirit into the wilderness to be tempted by the devil*" (Matthew 4:1). You filled him with the word of God and, though he was *led* to the crisis of temptation by your Spirit, he did not get sucked into sin, but triumphed by your word (Matthew 4:4, 7, 10). For this same grace, in all your leadings, we earnestly pray. Amen.[4]

This is what diligent biblical study looks like sometimes. It takes a thorough review of context, word studies, and consulting other Scriptures (like Deuteronomy 8, Luke 4, and James 1) so that Scripture interprets Scripture, as well as hard theological reflection that may run counterintuitive to assumptions (like the wrongheaded assumption that God would never test us) in order to properly understand a difficult text.

But what we must not do is change the actual words of Jesus. That's tantamount to sitting in authority above the Scriptures, exalting our opinions above God's Word, which is always wrong.

James reminds us that God does not tempt us to sin, but as Scripture elsewhere teaches, God does allow us to be tested. But even if in the midst of our tests we are tempted, these comforting words should give us hope:

No temptation has come upon you except what is common to humanity. But God is faithful; he will not allow you to be tempted beyond what you are able, but with the temptation he will also provide a way out so that you may be able to bear it.

1 Corinthians 10:13

8

Foreskins and Foolishness

One thing we can say for sure about God's Word, it is anything but boring. Perhaps no one exemplified this reality more than the most famous king of Israel, King David. The man's life was full of drama. In fact, I would suggest that David's life had more dramatic story lines in it than ten people's lives combined. He was truly a charismatic figure in the history of Israel, a man who was handsome, eloquent, crafty, intuitive, and winsome. A warrior, leader, prophet, king, and, just like you and me, a sinner.

His life was full of excitement. Even in his youthful days serving as a simple shepherd boy, he faced danger numerous times, protecting his sheep from lions and bears (1 Samuel 17:36). He grew up with seven older brothers, so you know there was likely some family rivalry along with all the stories and issues that would go with that.

As a young man, he was chosen by God to replace a disobedient King Saul, Israel's first king. However, the honor of that role was delayed because of the lengthy transition and drama that existed between the two. Saul's life was a mess. He disobeyed God's commands in battle, overstepped his role in attempting to assume priestly duties, and consulted a medium in direct opposition to the Law of Moses. He was filled with pride, greed, and jealousy as David became a nemesis to him.

The Lord's favor clearly fell on David. While serving King Saul, David battled the giant Philistine, Goliath, and with a simple slingshot, emerged victorious. David then proved himself to be a mighty warrior for the king, and the people sang, "Saul has killed his thousands, but David his tens of thousands" (1 Samuel 18:7). This did nothing but pour salt on the wounded relationship, and the Bible says that Saul looked at David with suspicion and jealousy because of this (1 Samuel 18:9).

One day, while David was playing his harp to ease the troubled soul of the king, Saul's jealousy led him to toss his javelin right at David not only once, but twice. Yet again, God protected David, and he escaped the danger. Saul saw that David was continually blessed with God's favor, and his fear of David gradually increased so much that he began to scheme. He decided to send David away and make him a commander in the army, hoping that eventually he might get killed. But this only made matters worse, because God's blessing was on David and he prospered, becoming even more popular among the people.

What was Saul to do now? Another idea came to mind. He promised David his daughter Merab's hand in marriage if he would go out and fight against the mighty Philistines again on Saul's behalf, this time calling it "the Lord's battles" so as to convince David of its importance. David was humbled, and he obediently went, and Saul sat hoping that the Philistines would defeat him, but it never happened. Unfortunately, when David returned victorious yet again, he found that his promised wife had already been given away to another man. The cruelty of Saul knew no bounds.

When Saul learned that his other daughter, Michal, loved David, he decided to give her away to David instead. But David still felt unworthy and called himself a "commoner," indicating that he didn't have the means or money to afford the "bride price," which was an ancient custom of the groom transferring money or property to the family of the bride. Then Saul came up with another plan, a rather bizarre one.

> Saul replied, "Say this to David: 'The king desires no other bride-price except a hundred Philistine foreskins, to take revenge on his enemies.'" Actually, Saul intended to cause David's death at the hands of the Philistines.
>
> 1 Samuel 18:25

Say what? Foreskins? Being the "uncircumcised" enemies of Israel that they were (and thus cast off from the blessings of the Abrahamic covenant, of which circumcision was a sign), the Philistines were once again to be the object of David's conquest. It was as if Saul was trying to slam David against a wall repeatedly, hoping that the odds would one day catch up with him and he would fall to the Philistines.

But because David had the Lord's favor, he once again prevailed, and as was a common custom in ancient battles, David and his men humiliated the Philistines by bringing not one hundred but two hundred mutilated and detached foreskins before Saul as the "price" for his daughter. He went above and beyond the expectation. Can you imagine? Such is the context of the ancient world. It did not seem to bother Michal because she apparently was in love with David. We have no record of her saying to her father, "I'm worth what? Two hundred foreskins?"

So with the debt more than paid, David and Michal married. Saul was a mental and emotional mess, and his heart got even darker.

> Saul realized that the Lord was with David and that his daughter Michal loved him, and he became even more afraid of David. As a result, Saul was David's enemy from then on. Every time the Philistine commanders came out to fight, David was more

successful than all of Saul's officers. So his name became well known.

1 Samuel 18:28–30

Over time, Saul decided he had enough, and he stopped with the discreet plans and simply ordered his son Jonathan to kill David. There was no more disguising his hatred for David. But David and Jonathan were best of friends, and Jonathan temporarily convinced his father not to sin in this way. But Saul's heart remained unchanged, and as David continued to win victories against the Philistines, Saul's craze-filled jealousy and rage flamed even higher.

As part of God's judgment on Saul, the Sovereign LORD would often allow an evil spirit to torment him. It is not as if the LORD was authoring evil, but rather he allowed evil to run its course on someone who was doing nothing but participating in evil.[1] God removed his protective hand from Saul while keeping his protective hand on David, and when the evil spirit began afflicting Saul, yet another spear headed David's way.

> Now an evil spirit sent from the LORD came on Saul as he was sitting in his palace holding a spear. David was playing the lyre, and Saul tried to pin David to the wall with the spear. As the spear struck the wall, David eluded Saul, ran away, and escaped that night. Saul sent agents to David's house to watch for him and kill him in the morning. But his wife Michal warned David, "If you don't escape tonight, you will be dead tomorrow!" So she lowered David from the window, and he fled and escaped.
>
> 1 Samuel 19:9–12

From that point on, David was on the run, and the rest of 1 Samuel is dedicated to what became a permanent estrangement between the two men. Indeed, one of the more bizarre episodes comes later in 1 Samuel 21, when David decided to enter into a Philistine city carrying the sword of Goliath (the Philistine giant whom he had slain). It was David's only weapon of protection, and according to David, there was "none like it" (1 Samuel 21:9).

David had retrieved the weapon from a priest who had kept it as a memorial to the Lord's victory over Israel's enemies.

Running from Saul and carrying the sword, he entered the Philistine city of Gath, which ironically was the hometown of the dead giant Goliath.[2] The fact is, it would be unlikely that Saul would ever think to find David there. His arrival was reported to the local Philistine king named Achish, and a rather strange scene unfolded. We pick up the story in verse 10.

> David fled that day from Saul's presence and went to King Achish of Gath. But Achish's servants said to him, "Isn't this David, the king of the land? Don't they sing about him during their dances: Saul has killed his thousands, but David his tens of thousands?"
>
> David took this to heart and became very afraid of King Achish of Gath, so he pretended to be insane in their presence. He acted like a madman around them, scribbling on the doors of the city gate and letting saliva run down his beard.
>
> 1 Samuel 21:10–13

I'm sure the Philistines were in shock. They *thought* they recognized David as the leader and warrior that he was known to be. However, something was really off. He was not acting like a kingly warrior, and why was he alone? Was this a trick? Was it even him?

Fearing they knew who he was, David began to scribble and drool, putting on quite a performance. (Apparently the man was not only a shepherd, a warrior, and a harpist, he was a talented actor as well. When you are on the run, I guess you will do anything.) David seemed to be improvising on the spot, coming up with his best solution without seeking the Lord's help. But when we refuse to seek the Lord, we go only as far as our weakened and sinful flesh will take us.

The response of the Philistine king is hysterical.

> "Look! You can see the man is crazy," Achish said to his servants. "Why did you bring him to me? Do I have such a shortage of crazy

people that you brought this one to act crazy around me? Is this one going to come into my house?"

1 Samuel 21:14–15

I must admit, there are times when I have felt like Achish, surrounded by craziness. You too? Life is full of challenging people. But on a more serious note, what David was doing was no laughing matter. In the culture of that day, drooling on your beard was considered an intolerable indignity.[3]

As funny as this story is, and as creative as David was in deceiving the enemy, he seemed to be stooping to all kinds of lows to escape from Saul, to the point of losing his dignity. Earlier in the previous chapter, he lied to the priest who ended up giving him Goliath's sword. (David claimed he was on a mission from King Saul.) And here David was seeking refuge *with the enemy*, and in order to avoid the worst, decided to act insane.

You might wonder, Why did David seemingly take matters into his own hands instead of trusting and asking the LORD what to do? Did the enemy show more promise of protecting him than the LORD? Why did David rely on his own human intuition to make sense of his life?

This is often our temptation, isn't it? We do all we can in our own flesh to try and figure out how to overcome our trials, when all along we should be seeking God's heart, trusting in him, searching the Scriptures, praying, seeking godly counsel, and waiting on the Lord.

Stories like this have their place in the Bible. I believe first and foremost it shows us that nothing will thwart God's plan (Job 42:2), and that even though we often seek to take matters into our own hands, God's plans are the ones that will prevail. The purposes, plans, and promises of God are trustworthy and true. God will accomplish his sovereign will, because his glory is attached to it.

In the end, David escaped Saul's evil intent and became king. Saul was wounded in battle with the Philistines, and fell on his own sword, committing suicide.

David went on to be the mighty and powerful king that he was called to be, but still faltered and failed miserably when he acted out of his flesh. Adultery, murder, David would grieve the LORD many times. But David would confess, repent, and seek God's heart, and God's grace would cover him. It would be from David's ancestral line that our Savior would emerge, the One who provides the ultimate cure for the insanity that is our sin.

God's plans will always prevail, both in *spite* of us, and *because* of us.

9

The Finger on the Wall

≡ DANIEL 5 ≡

Do you ever wonder how we got certain sayings or idioms? "Don't count your chickens before they hatch," for example, came from a sonnet written in 1570 by Thomas Howell.[1] It is good advice aimed at keeping us from boasting too soon or assuming too much. "Don't toss the baby out with the bathwater" has been traced to a 1512 German satirical work known as *Appeal to Fools*. The advice communicates the idea that we should not "discard something valuable along with something undesirable."[2]

A number of well-known expressions have roots in the Bible, including these five.[3]

1. *"Like a lamb to the slaughter"*—Undoubtedly comes from Isaiah 53:7, in talking of the Messiah who would be slain.

2. *"A leopard cannot change its spots"*—From Jeremiah 13:23, when God threatens Israel with exile and asks rhetorically, "Can the Ethiopian change his skin or the leopard change his spots?" (ESV).

3. *"Fall by the wayside"*—taken from Luke 8:5 in reference
   to the parable of the sower, and how some seeds did not
   land on good soil but rather on the path where they were
   crushed and gobbled up by birds. We use the phrase to
   communicate the idea that something was sidelined, put
   aside, or discarded out of bounds such that it is no longer
   paid attention to.

4. *"A sign of the times"*—Jesus used the phrase in Matthew
   16:3 to rebuke the Pharisees and Sadducees who discerned
   the weather forecast by looking at the sky but were unable
   to exercise spiritual discernment and recognize Jesus as
   the Messiah. They could not read the "signs of the times."

5. *"An eye for an eye"*—I discussed this expression in my
   book *The Most Misused Verses in the Bible*. The phrase
   comes from Exodus 21:24, where God is setting limits on
   levels of punishment for various crimes. The verse should
   not be used as a proof text for personal vengeance or to
   legitimize equal harm in the form of retaliation. Rather, it
   was a judicial principle in Israel that was meant to teach
   that the punishment must fit the crime.

Another saying worthy of investigation due to its unique circumstances is *"the writing is on the wall."* Today, it communicates that
something is coming to its conclusion. It is the idea that the end
is near, someone is about to be fired, or the season is almost over.

In the book of Daniel, the expression had far-reaching consequences for a pagan king who was about to lose his kingdom and
his life. The story starts in the sixth century BC, when the prophet
Daniel and his fellow Israelites are taken from the Holy Land and
brought to Babylon under King Nebuchadnezzar.

Daniel becomes famous for interpreting dreams, a unique ability the Lord gave him as a prophet of God's people. In Daniel 2,
Daniel is able to interpret a dream that King Nebuchadnezzar has
when his own astrologers, magicians, and soothsayers could not.
As a result, Daniel is promoted and becomes a ruler of a province

in Babylon. Through miracles and his ability to interpret dreams, Daniel and his friends are given a place of high honor and respect even in exile, and Nebuchadnezzar recognizes that God's spirit is in Daniel, calling him the "chief of the magicians" (Daniel 4:9).

After his profession of faith and subsequent death (Daniel 4:34–36),[4] King Nebuchadnezzar's kingdom exchanges hands until Belshazzar and his father become co-regents several decades later. Daniel has since become an old man, perhaps in his early eighties.[5]

Even though Daniel is still revered in the land, Belshazzar does not believe in Israel's God. He has no regard for the LORD and, in fact, will do blasphemous and dishonorable things with the sacred relics of Israel's now destroyed temple in Jerusalem.

> King Belshazzar held a great feast for a thousand of his nobles and drank wine in their presence. Under the influence of the wine, Belshazzar gave orders to bring in the gold and silver vessels that his predecessor Nebuchadnezzar had taken from the temple in Jerusalem . . . and the king and his nobles, wives, and concubines drank from them. They drank the wine and praised their gods made of gold and silver, bronze, iron, wood, and stone.
>
> Daniel 5:1–4

The Babylonians were warring with the Medo-Persians when this "great feast" was taking place. We are not told why it was held, but many surmise it was designed to boost morale. Lavish feasts were common in Babylon, but this particular one was quickly interrupted by something freakishly scary. Here, then, is where our famous phrase finds its origins.

> At that moment the fingers of a man's hand appeared and began writing on the plaster of the king's palace wall next to the lampstand. As the king watched the hand that was writing, his face turned pale, and his thoughts so terrified him that he soiled himself and his knees knocked together.
>
> Daniel 5:5–6

Talk about creepy. No person, not even an arm, just the fingers of a hand appear, and they start writing on the plaster of the palace walls. This sounds like something from a Hollywood movie. Nevertheless, the king is in total panic mode, turns pale, and even loses control of his body.

He then calls out for his enchanters, mediums, and soothsayers to have them read what was written on the wall, but none of them could do it. This was beyond them, but the queen knew who to call. She knew about Daniel's reputation and told the king, "In the days of your predecessor he was found to have insight, intelligence, and wisdom like the wisdom of the gods" (5:11).

Daniel was brought in and promised rewards, including the third-highest rank in the kingdom, if he could interpret the writing. Daniel's response is fitting:

> "You may keep your gifts and give your rewards to someone else; however, I will read the inscription for the king and make the interpretation known to him."
>
> Daniel 5:17

Daniel then proceeds to give the king a history lesson, reminding him of how the LORD gave Nebuchadnezzar the power he had to dominate, destroy, and take captive anyone he wanted until the day the LORD humbled him. Nebuchadnezzar's pride and arrogance brought on the LORD's judgment, and he was made to go insane for many years until "he acknowledged that the Most High God is ruler over the human kingdoms and sets anyone he wants over them" (5:21).[6]

One would think that the humbling of the previous king would have an effect on those who followed, but this was definitely not the case. Daniel then launches into a formal indictment of Belshazzar for his lack of humility and desecration of the sacred vessels from the temple in Jerusalem. He reads the writing on the wall, which in Aramaic reads, "*Mene, Mene, Tekel, and Parsin.*" Daniel explained,

This is the interpretation of the message: "Mene" means that God has numbered the days of your kingdom and brought it to an end. "Tekel" means that you have been weighed on the balance and found deficient. "Peres" [singular of Parsin] means that your kingdom has been divided and given to the Medes and Persians.

Daniel 5:26–28

In other words, your days are over. And on October 16, 539 BC, the same night all of this happened, "Darius the Mede" and his army invaded the city and killed the king, bringing an end to the Babylonian rule.[7] Talk about quick, immediate, and on point—when God says you are done, you are done.

The reason why this "writing on the wall" story is in the Bible is to remind us that God is providentially in control and is working out his purposes in the world and in our lives as well. He is sovereign over people and nations, for as Daniel wrote earlier,

May the name of God be praised forever and ever, for wisdom and power belong to him. He changes the times and seasons; he removes kings and establishes kings.

Daniel 2:20–21

We can trust our God. He is always in control. He even sets up and appoints those who are in charge of the affairs of the world (see Romans 13:1). Though many are like Belshazzar and do not regard God, nevertheless God is in control. Even though the world is full of evil, the King of Kings and Lord of Lords will one day come and vanquish evil from the earth once and for all. His name is Jesus, and Daniel, in his prophetic vision of the second coming and his future earthly reign, said of him,

He was given dominion, and glory, and a kingdom; so that those of every people, nation, and language should serve him. His dominion is an everlasting dominion that will not pass away, and his kingdom is one that will not be destroyed.

Daniel 7:14

10

Jesus and
an Unfortunate Fig Tree

MARK 11:12–14, 20–25

ew things gripped Jesus' heart like the hypocrisy he saw in the leaders of Israel. They looked good on the outside with all of their performance-based religiosity, but deep in their souls a spiritual darkness dominated their motives. They were committed to man-made rules, man-made religion, and man-centered showiness. The prophet Isaiah described them perfectly when he prophesied hundreds of years earlier:

> The Lord said: These people approach me with their speeches to honor me with lip-service—yet their hearts are far from me, and human rules direct their worship of me.
>
> Isaiah 29:13

The Pharisees and scribes had managed to corrupt the systemic religion of the nation of Israel, and though there truly were exceptions to this, the nation as a whole was spiritually wandering and following the guidance of their corrupt leadership. The temple was especially corrupt; all kinds of inappropriate commerce, thievery, spiritual fraud, and exclusion took place there.

Mark records for us an event that happened in the last week of Jesus' life that on the surface puzzles us until we have fully grasped the aforementioned context. On more than one occasion, Jesus cleansed the temple of the corrupt money changers that were there taking advantage of the people who came to offer sacrifices and present their offering to the LORD.[1]

Sandwiched around that final cleansing is an encounter with a promising but fruitless fig tree that quickly becomes an object lesson for two theological truths concerning Israel and the need for faith.

Our setting is simple: Jesus arrives in Jerusalem (on what we call Palm Sunday) on a donkey, amidst great crowds, to the cheers of "Hosanna, blessed is he who comes in the name of the Lord" (v. 9). At the end of that great day, he peeks into the temple and doesn't like what he sees, but he has to wait until the next morning to deal with it. So he leaves and spends the night in nearby Bethany.

The next morning Jesus gets up, likely skips breakfast, and makes a beeline back to the temple to deal with the corruption he saw the night before. However, before he arrives, he notices something strange.

> The next day when they went out from Bethany, [Jesus] was hungry. Seeing in the distance a fig tree with leaves, he went to find out if there was anything on it. When he came to it, he found nothing but leaves; for it was not the season for figs. He said to it, "May no one ever eat fruit from you again!" And his disciples heard it.
>
> Mark 11:12–14

At first glance this seems a little weird. What's with the cursing of a helpless, unarmed tree? This seems a little out of character when you look at it on the surface, but some history will help.

Many of the prophetic writings in the Old Testament often used the vine or the fig tree to illustrate the spiritual life of Israel (cf.

Isaiah 5:1–7; Jeremiah 8:13; 24:1–8; Hosea 9:10; Joel 1:7). Fig trees were common there. They were part of the abundant Promised Land that God had given to his people.

They were tall and shady, fruitful—a place where people gathered. One may remember that when Jesus called Nathaniel to be his disciple, he was sitting under a fig tree. So the tree was a symbol of blessing and God's favor—a sign of fruitful abundance. But when Jesus heads toward Jerusalem, he's surprised when he sees a fig tree off in the distance with leaves on it. Apparently, this tree was blooming prematurely—it had leaves on it a month or two ahead of time.

Now, when fig trees bloom (twice every year), there is always fruit. Since Jesus was a little hungry, the sight of a fig tree was promising. But when he gets closer to the tree, he sees leaves but no fruit. It looked great from a distance, but when seen up close, it is empty and fruitless, just like the corrupt leadership of Israel (and perhaps, to a certain degree, the nation as a whole).

Seen on the outside, things look good, but a closer look at the heart reveals something very different. Jesus then decides to use this tree as an object lesson, and he puts a curse on the tree (which the disciples heard). Matthew tells us that the tree withered right away (21:19), and the disciples were stunned.

Jesus then proceeds to the temple and clears it out, overturning tables and chairs and driving out those who were participating in its corruption. Much like the fig tree, the chief priests and scribes that authorized the corrupt commerce were simply worthless and spiritually bankrupt frauds. Cursed men whose end is death, much like the tree.

After leaving the temple, Jesus goes back to where he's staying. But the next day, they pass by the cursed tree one more time.

> Early in the morning, as they were passing by, they saw the fig tree withered from the roots up. Then Peter remembered and said to him, "Rabbi, look! The fig tree that you cursed has withered."
>
> Mark 11:20–21

Jesus uses that withered fig tree to teach yet another spiritual truth—the power of faith-filled prayer. You see, that's what was missing amongst God's people, and especially the leadership—faith. Faith was missing. Instead, Jesus is finding fake religion, corruption, going through the motions, and a fruitlessness that will only end in death and destruction. When there is no faith, there is no fruit, and faith without works is dead (James 2:17).

Seizing upon that idea, Jesus wants to capitalize on the theme of faith and relate it to the importance of having faith in the context of prayer.

> Jesus replied to them, "Have faith in God. Truly I tell you, if anyone says to this mountain, 'Be lifted up and thrown into the sea,' and does not doubt in his heart, but believes that what he says will happen, it will be done for him. Therefore I tell you, everything you pray and ask for—believe that you have received it and it will be yours."
>
> Mark 11:22–24

This in itself is quite a perplexing statement that has the potential to be misunderstood. Obviously, Jesus is not giving us a blank check when it comes to prayer (as if he is teaching, "fill in what you want and you'll get it as long as you *believe* you'll get it"). This is because God's sovereignty and purposes will always naturally be a part of truly effectual prayer. For John elsewhere teaches us . . .

> This is the confidence we have before him: *If we ask anything according to his will*, he hears us. And if we know that he hears whatever we ask, we know that we have what we have asked of him.
>
> 1 John 5:14–15, emphasis mine

So the qualifier is *"asking according to his will."* And the main point Jesus is teaching is on the necessity of having faith in the context of prayer. That kind of prayer has the power to move mountains (metaphorically speaking).

This is a powerful reminder of the importance of living a faith-filled life and practicing the spiritual disciplines with that same God-focused, God-glorifying faith, not merely a fake faith centered on the will of man (like the lives of the Pharisees, chief priests, and scribes).

So Jesus is not arbitrarily making a habit of randomly cursing fig trees if they so happen to disappoint or frustrate him while he's looking for breakfast. No, he used that tree to warn us of the dangers of fruitlessness and to remind us of the need to live by faith so that our lives will produce the fruit of faith-filled prayer.

He used one tree to teach us two spiritual truths so that we don't end up being nothing but a religious show, much like the temple. He's looking for faith—faith that produces fruit. Do we have it?

11

A Message from God

In Psalm 44, the psalmist begins with a victory song about how the LORD has delivered God's people from their enemies in the past. Stories of God's deliverance were passed down from generation to generation, recounting God's faithfulness to triumph over the enemy. Even in Israel's victories, the psalmist knows that ultimately this has come from God.

> Through you we push down our foes;
>> through your name we tread down those who rise up
>>> against us.
> For not in my bow do I trust,
>> nor can my sword save me.
> But you have saved us from our foes
>> and have put to shame those who hate us.
> In God we have boasted continually,
>> and we will give thanks to your name forever.
>>> Psalm 44:5–8 ESV

Though the psalmist will then speak with perplexity at their recent string of defeats, toward the end of the psalm, he returns to the hope of future victory based on the aforementioned past success, for he knows that when God chooses to deliver, it will happen and can be quite dramatic. In fact, not only does God deliver his people, but he seemingly is not afraid to put Israel's enemies to *shame*, as a form of judgment upon them (Psalm 44:7).

You may remember from the introduction to this book that God can exercise his judgment on sin whenever and however he pleases. He is holy, and until we understand how offensive human sin is toward his holiness, we will never fully appreciate the right God has to bring justice to the world in the manner, means, and timing of his own choosing.

Having said this, we now turn to a story in the book of Judges that reminds us that God's judgment on his enemies who refuse to repent of their idolatry can take many forms—even to the point of putting them to shame.

In Judges, God's people, the Israelites, have settled into the Promised Land under the leadership of Joshua. But upon Joshua's death (and slightly before), Israel begins to fall away from the commitment they made with God at Mount Sinai. Their allegiance to his commands begins to wane.

In settling in the land, they do not completely obey God's command to cleanse the land of the evil, idolatrous Canaanites. Further, they disobey God's commands by intermarrying with these pagan peoples who worshiped other gods and adopting their idolatry. They reject God's authority, pursue their own flesh, and sin against God. The daunting announcement in the book of Judges is that "in those days there was no king in Israel. Everyone did what was right in his own eyes" (17:6 ESV).

Israel's idolatry and spiritual adultery lead God to send them into oppression, first by the king of Mesopotamia, who oppresses them for eight years until Israel cries out and God delivers them through a judge named Othniel (Caleb's younger brother), who then defeats the enemy king in battle. Forty years of peace prevails until Israel once again does evil in the sight of the LORD. As a judgment, Israel is given over to the hands of a Moabite king named Eglon, who wrangles up a coalition of Ammonites and Amalekites to help him defeat Israel. This time the oppression lasts eighteen years until Israel cries out to the LORD for help.[1]

Once again, God raises up a judge as a deliverer, this time a man by the name of Ehud. The text says that Ehud was a left-handed Benjamite (being left-handed had some strategic advantage in battle). Ehud makes a double-edged sword that is about eighteen inches long, and he hides it under his right thigh. He then leads an Israelite group to the Moabite king to pay "tribute" (taxes and fees), which was a regular practice for nations that were subservient to other nations. Scripture describes the gory details of what happens next.

> And he presented the tribute to Eglon king of Moab. Now Eglon was a very fat man. And when Ehud had finished presenting the tribute, he sent away the people who carried the tribute. But he himself turned back at the idols near Gilgal and said, "I have a secret message for you, O king." And he commanded, "Silence." And all his attendants went out from his presence. And Ehud came to him as he was sitting alone in his cool roof chamber. And Ehud said, "I have a message from God for you." And he arose from his seat. And Ehud reached with his left hand, took the sword from his right thigh, and thrust it into his belly. And the hilt also went in after the blade, and the fat closed over the blade, for he did not pull the sword out of his belly; and the dung came out. Then Ehud went out into the porch and closed the doors of the roof chamber behind him and locked them.
>
> Judges 3:17–23 ESV

Yes, that really happened. Ehud was a little clever, a little deceitful, and determined to carry out his mission.[2] He tricks the fat king into giving him a private meeting, a meeting away from all the king's attendants in a special room of the king's chambers. He has a "secret message" in the form of a knife. It is here that the assassination takes place. Apparently, "the leader of the enemies must be disposed of before the occupying army can be routed."[3]

But it's the graphic description of the killing that makes us wonder, Why is *that* in the Bible? The knife goes in and never comes out. If I were there, I'd be saying, "You know what? You can have that knife. I'm good. I'll make another one." Surely, the more details we have, the more authentic this story seems. But are there other reasons why this is so disgustingly graphic? Perhaps. Let's read on.

> When he had gone, the servants came, and when they saw that the doors of the roof chamber were locked, they thought, "Surely he is relieving himself in the closet of the cool chamber." And they waited till they were embarrassed. But when he still did not open the doors of the roof chamber, they took the key and opened them, and there lay their lord dead on the floor.
>
> Judges 3:24–25 esv

For us, the reader, the graphic description of the killing is eclipsed by the humor that comes next. Ehud is clearly given a lot of time to escape, because when the attendants discover the doors locked, they wait outside ("till they were embarrassed"), thinking the king is in there going to the bathroom. Why would they think that? Maybe they know his gastrointestinal habits well, *or maybe* they smelled the spilled dung from the assassination. Yuck!

This may explain why we are told about the disgusting parts of this story. They let us know how Ehud had time to escape and go back to muster up the Israelite army for the eventual return ambush that would rout ten thousand Moabite soldiers and give Israel the deliverance that God had planned for them—a deliverance that will bring another eighty years of peace before Israel gets into trouble again.

So in this story there may be good reasons why the Bible gives us the humorous and disgusting details of a pagan king's death and the deliverance of God's people that ensued from it. It argues for its believability and authenticity, and it helps us understand how the process of Israel's deliverance came about (in all of its *perfect timing*). The evil king lay dead in his dung. Truly, as the psalmist would later write, God's enemies are "put to shame" (Psalm 6:10 esv).

12

An Ear Is Cut Off

= JOHN 18; MATTHEW 26 =

The apostle Peter is one of my favorite biblical characters. A fisherman by trade, Peter was a hardworking man with a bold personality. Read the gospel accounts and you quickly see he was a man with firm convictions, passionate emotions, an inquisitive spirit, and a boldness that set him apart from others. Before he became the outspoken leader of the twelve apostles and the keynote speaker at Pentecost, Peter went by the name of *Simon* (Greek) or *Simeon* (Hebrew), until he met Jesus, who subsequently renamed him Peter (which means "rock" in Aramaic).

Peter's family context is listed in the Bible—his father's name was Jonas, Jonah (Matthew 16:17), or John (John 1:42), and he had a brother named Andrew, who was the first to introduce him to Jesus (John 1:40–42). Originally from the town of Bethsaida, they eventually moved to Capernaum, the most important seaside village on the northern end of the Sea of Galilee. There the boys were active as fishermen, and it was there where Jesus met them and called them (along with John) to follow him.

Jesus himself made Capernaum into his ministry base and hometown during his Galilean ministry. Here, Jesus also called Matthew (or "Levi") the tax collector to join him. Though the people of Capernaum did not believe in Jesus, he still performed some miraculous healings there, including healing a Roman centurion's servant (Matthew 8:5–13).

Interestingly, Jesus also miraculously cured Peter's mother-in-law from a fever (Matthew 8:14–15), which tells us even more information about Peter—that he was married. Apparently, later, during his travels as an apostle spreading the gospel, Peter brought his wife along with him (1 Corinthians 9:5). Not only was he the leader of the Twelve and "pillar" of the church (Galatians 2:9), Peter also wrote the books of 1 and 2 Peter.

What especially stands out about Peter was his unique relationship with Jesus. He had a deep love for and loyalty to Jesus. Surely there were moments of weakness (like when he denied Christ three times on the night of Christ's betrayal), but few could doubt that Peter was a sold-out follower of Christ who was unafraid to take risks and speak up even before he had reasoned things out in his mind.

Peter was bold with Jesus on many occasions. He was the first to call Jesus "the Christ, the Son of the Living God" (Matthew 16:16–17), and the only one who got out of the boat in the middle of a stormy night and attempted to walk on water to get to Jesus (Matthew 14:28–30). Later, when Jesus spoke about dying, Peter pulled Jesus aside and sought to straighten him out (Matthew 16:21–22). But this was a mistake, as Jesus rebuked Peter for speaking out of turn, even identifying the agenda Peter had as coming from Satan (an agenda that sought to keep Jesus from his appointed sacrificial death).

During the Last Supper when Jesus began to wash the disciples' feet, it was Peter who initially refused, saying, "You shall never wash my feet" (John 13:8), thinking that it was beneath Jesus to do such a menial task. Corrected by Jesus yet again, Peter quickly said he wanted not only his feet washed, but his hands and head too. Only later would Peter understand the significance of the spiritual washing Jesus was referring to in this symbolic act.[1]

The Gospels include many other "Peter moments," if you will. Quite dramatically, near the end of Jesus' life, Peter actually drew his sword in the garden of Gethsemane when Jesus was being arrested by the Roman soldiers and temple police. Led to Jesus by Judas, his betrayer, the soldiers came with lanterns, torches, and weapons to take Jesus prisoner. But Peter would have none of it.

> Then Jesus, knowing all that would happen to him, came forward and said to them, "Whom do you seek?" They answered him, "Jesus of Nazareth." Jesus said to them, "I am he." Judas, who betrayed him, was standing with them. When Jesus said to them, "I am he," they drew back and fell to the ground. So he asked them again, "Whom do you seek?" And they said, "Jesus of Nazareth." Jesus answered, "I told you that I am he. So, if you seek me, let these men go." This was to fulfill the word that he had spoken: "Of those whom you gave me I have lost not one."
>
> John 18:4–9 ESV

None of this was surprising to Jesus. He knew this was God's plan, and he was willing to submit to it. But in the process, he wanted to make sure his disciples were protected, so he made the soldiers specifically state whom they were seeking. The Synoptic Gospel accounts tell us about the kiss of Judas meant to identify Jesus (Matthew 26:48–49; Mark 14:44–45; Luke 22:47–48), and after they verbalize who they were seeking—Jesus of Nazareth—he says to them, "I am he." In the original Greek, though, Jesus simply says, "I am." The words "I am" have profound significance, for coming from Jesus' lips, they are the words of his self-identification as none other than God himself (see John 8:24, 28, 58). No wonder the soldiers drew back and fell to the ground. This voice was the voice of power—the voice of their Creator (see John 1:3; Colossians 1:16; Hebrews 1:2).

But before they can secure their captive, Peter impetuously decides once again to take matters into his own hands.

> Then Simon Peter, having a sword, drew it and struck the high priest's servant and cut off his right ear. (The servant's name was Malchus.) So Jesus said to Peter, "Put your sword into its sheath; shall I not drink the cup that the Father has given me?"
>
> John 18:10–11

There is no doubt what Peter was aiming for, and it wasn't the guy's ear. Luckily the guy ducked out of the way, or he would have lost his head. Interestingly, John gives us the name of the servant—Malchus, which once again argues for the authenticity of these kinds of accounts. In Dr. Luke's gospel, Jesus reattaches and heals Malchus's ear (Luke 22:51), but not before rebuking Peter once again.

Jesus says, "No more of this!" (Luke 22:51), and tells Peter to put away his sword (John 18:11). Jesus states that he could call on the Father to send legions of angels to protect him if he wanted (Matthew 26:53), but that wouldn't be appropriate, because all this was prophesied in the Scriptures to happen. He asks the rhetorical question, "Shall I not drink the cup that the Father has given me?" (John 18:11).

What Jesus is referring to is the "cup of wrath" that would come from God the Father, as Jesus would die on a cross to atone for sin. His death would absorb the wrath of God, as it was God's plan to make Jesus into a substitutionary atoning sacrifice for our sins.

Once again, Peter unknowingly finds himself in the same position he was in earlier when he unwittingly opposed God's plan to send Jesus to the cross. But rather than let him start an all-out war in the garden, Jesus took matters (and the servant's ear) into his own hands and performed a miracle in front of them all. You'd think the miracle would have made them all reconsider what they were doing and to whom they were doing it, but no, it did not deter them. Again, this was God's plan.

The fact that they did not arrest Peter for his actions points to the protection of Jesus over his disciples in that moment, even when they made mistakes. They were secure in God's hands—which is good news for us when we make mistakes from time to time. Eventually, Jesus is led away and taken to the Jewish leaders for a fraudulent trial in the middle of the night.

I suggest there are several reasons this story is in the Bible.

First, the details of the account, including the name of the wounded servant, argue once again for the historicity and authenticity of the account. Second, it seems clear that the gospel writers capture this event to show us that the disciples (and, in this case, Peter) didn't fully understand the mission of Jesus at first. It was only after the resurrection and the giving of the Holy Spirit that these events made sense to them—that it had to happen for the Scriptures and God's saving plan to be fulfilled.

Third, this story is undoubtedly in the Bible to show us how much control Jesus had over the situation. Though the soldiers tied his hands and led him away, he went to the cross willingly, and if he wanted to, he could have called thousands upon thousands of angels to save him. Human authorities with clubs and swords wouldn't have stood a chance against angel armies. But again, that wasn't God's plan.

We often think we know best when it comes to how our lives ought to go. But we must remember that our lives are in Christ's hands, his sovereign will for us is perfect, and only in submitting our will to the will of God (like Jesus did in the garden) will we find the solutions to the middle-of-the-night battles we face.

13

Jeremiah's Linen Underwear

There are places in Scripture where God illustrates spiritual truths in beautiful and endearing ways, such as the day when Christ will reign on the earth at his second coming and we're told there will be abundant peace on earth, even among the animal kingdom. Here, the "wolf will dwell with the lamb, and the leopard will lie down with the goat. The calf, the young lion, and the fattened calf will be together, and a child will lead them" (Isaiah 11:6). It's a picturesque scene of tranquility and peacefulness with the Lord Jesus himself present and reigning.

In other places in Scripture, God uses graphic illustrations and object lessons to illicit realism, sober-mindedness, humility, and eventually repentance from us as we see how God's people should see their sin before a holy God.

In the days of the prophet Jeremiah, the southern Israelite kingdom of Judah had forsaken the LORD. Idol worship, child sacrifices, adultery, and rampant injustice were but a few of Judah's sins that warranted judgment from God. God had raised up Jeremiah to preach a message of repentance for his people, but they refused to listen, so judgment would come. Throughout his life Jeremiah would not only be rejected by God's people, but also would endure threats, humiliation, trials, being put into stocks, and even thrown into a pit by these same people he dearly loved.

In Jeremiah 13, God chooses to illustrate creatively the spiritual condition of his people by asking Jeremiah to act out a prophetic word that would describe Judah's spiritual state. Jeremiah is told to go and buy a linen waistband (a piece of undergarment or underwear). The "intimacy" of this clothing was to represent the spiritual intimacy that God desired to have with his people who were designed to "cling to him" in a covenant relationship. They were claimed by God and saved so that "they might be my people for my fame, praise, and glory" (13:11).

But they did not obey and they did not listen. They had become altogether filthy before God, so Jeremiah was told to buy and wear this linen underwear but to never wash it (v. 1). Eventually this undergarment would be soiled, stinky, and anything else you could imagine underwear might become after being unwashed for a long period of time.

But it was about to get worse. Jeremiah is told to take the soiled garment, journey to the Euphrates River (in Babylon where Judah will eventually be exiled to), and hide the garment in the crevice of a rock. This is no small journey either, but one that would take him through all kinds of rough climate and hundreds of miles of terrain. By the time he got there to hide it in the rock, the condition of the linen would be reprehensible. But if that weren't enough, Jeremiah was told to leave it there for a long time, only to go and fetch it again.

A long time later the Lord said to me, "Go at once to the Euphrates and get the underwear that I commanded you to hide there." So I went to the Euphrates and dug up the underwear and got it from the place where I had hidden it, but it was ruined—of no use at all.

Jeremiah 13:6–7

Linen underwear was the perfect choice. Originally, it would have been beautiful when first purchased, and would serve as a reminder of Israel's priestly calling to be representatives of the LORD to the whole earth, since priests dressed in linen.[1] But over time, soiled without washing, the linen would break down, and when placed in a rock next to a river, where there is a lot of moisture, it would eventually begin to rot.

Spiritually speaking, Judah had become worthless to God, like a nasty pair of rotten linen underwear that was soiled and disgusting—unusable. It would be nothing to brag about, and the LORD makes a poignant declaration.

> This is what the LORD says: Just like this I will ruin the great pride of both Judah and Jerusalem. These evil people, who refuse to listen to me, who follow the stubbornness of their own hearts, and who have followed other gods to serve and bow in worship—they will be like this underwear, of no use at all.
>
> Jeremiah 13:9–10

So add this to the list of things Jeremiah had to endure in his life. Shame, reproach, and rotten underwear, all illustrative of the spiritual condition of Judah that God looked upon when he looked at his people. The thought of the filthy underwear is designed to disgust us so that we might feel a portion of what God feels when he sees his people compromised by the world around them. Instead of living for his fame, his praise, and his glory, we can become altogether worthless to *God's purposes* when we prostitute ourselves to the lusts and trappings of worldliness that only leave us soiled, filthy, and unusable.

In this way, the lesson is clear. We were designed to have an intimate, close, saving relationship with God, and to be used for his kingdom purposes. But unrepentant sin can corrupt and soil one's life, rendering us unusable in many instances. Our fellowship is shattered, and we distance ourselves from God (like living in exile). Yet genuine repentance will bring forth a spiritual cleansing, a washing that restores our fellowship with God and makes us ready to be used for God's intended purposes.

In many ways, this sounds much like what Paul said about the Corinthians, who prior to their salvation were corrupt and worthless, but now due to the work of the Holy Spirit in their lives, had been washed, set apart, and justified before a holy God (1 Corinthians 6:9–11). It is this kind of spiritually washed people who were bought at a price, set apart, and designed to bring God glory (1 Corinthians 6:20).

So let us leave the nasty, filthy, rotten life of sin behind. It is not a life worth wearing.

14

The Nephilim: Who Were They?

≡ GENESIS 6:1–4 ≡

There are times when the Bible presents us with limited information that can lead us into a conundrum. For example, in Genesis we read this:

> When mankind began to multiply on the earth and daughters were born to them, the sons of God saw that the daughters of mankind were beautiful, and they took any they chose as wives for themselves. And the LORD said, "My Spirit will not remain with mankind forever, because they are corrupt. Their days will be 120 years." The Nephilim were on the earth both in those days and afterward, when the sons of God came to the daughters of mankind, who bore children to them. They were the powerful men of old, the famous men.
>
> Genesis 6:1–4

The question is—who were the Nephilim of Genesis 6? In a period of increasing corruption on the face of the earth prior to the flood, there existed a group of people known as the Nephilim.

The name stems from the Hebrew word *naphal*, which means "to fall."[1] The concept is that they were "fallen ones" or even "giants" (the latter term stemming from the Greek and Latin translation of the Hebrew, which uses the word *gigantes*). But what are we truly referring to here? Gigantic "fallen" (i.e., "sinful") people? Or is it something else—something truly out of the ordinary?

The answer is not so simple. The scholarly views are many and varied. Verse 4 tells us they were "powerful men of old, the famous men." This seems to suggest they are merely natural men who had a reputation of being powerful and strong warriors, and due to their violent nature may have contributed to the corruption of the whole earth that God would eventually judge with a flood (even though at this point he only decides to limit the lifespan).

But wait, they are also said to be the sons of God and the daughters of men. And the problem that plagues every biblical scholar is the question: Who are the "sons of God" and "the daughters of men"? The reason this is questionable is because the phrase "sons of God" is found elsewhere in the Bible and used to refer either to godly people in covenant with God (Deuteronomy 14:1; Hosea 1:10) or to angels. That's right, *angels* (cf. Job 1:6; 2:1; 38:7; Psalm 29:1; 89:6). And if it is angels, this crosses the line into creepy, like some Hollywood movie.

Unfortunately, there has been little scholarly consensus on whether we are referring to angels or natural men. Even the ancient Jewish rabbis who predate the days of the early church fathers were divided on it. Some said they were demons who cohabitated with human women, violating God's natural order of things and producing a superhuman demigod-like species of people who were destroyed by God in the flood. But I tend to disagree with this.

Old Testament scholar Gleason Archer calls this view a "curious intrusion of pagan superstition that has no basis at all in the rest of Scripture."[2] Further, Archer suggests that if we concede these were supernatural beings (either evil demons or godly angels), we have some unique problems.

If they were minions of Satan, that is fallen angels, then they could not have been referred to as "sons of God." Demons of hell would never be so designated in Scripture. Nor could they have been angels of God, since God's angels always live in total obedience to Him and have no other yearning or desire but to do God's will and glorify His name. A sordid involvement with godless young women would therefore be completely out of character for angels as "sons of God."[3]

A further problem with the "sons of God" view as angels or de-mons is that nothing in the context of Genesis 6 suggests we should interpret it in a supernatural manner. If anything, the context suggests we may be dealing with the godly line of Seth (Adam's son) that called upon the LORD (Genesis 4:26) and whose lineage is traced all throughout Genesis 5. This would mean the "sons of God" are to be potentially seen as godly descendants of Seth, who made a huge mistake by intermarrying ungodly women ("daugh-ters of mankind," likely Cain's descendants), which brought about an entirely corrupt generation of offspring (see the next verse of Genesis 6:5) worthy of God's wrath (and therefore, the flood).[4]

Lastly, one final blow to the supernatural-beings theory is the idea that angels are "spirits" that do not normally have human bodies and do not possess human DNA. Further, Jesus taught in the Gospels that angels do not marry and are not given in marriage (Matthew 12:22; Mark 12:25), so they do not reproduce, because spiritual beings are not capable of doing that.

But what about the places in the Bible where we see examples of angels being able to take on some kind of *temporary* human form (e.g., Genesis 19:1–3; Hebrews 13:2), even though it is often the exception to the rule concerning angels? Could they have been fallen angels who took on temporary form in order to reproduce and corrupt humanity, even though in Scripture we only see "good" angels allowed to take such a form? Now you can see the problem. For every theory, there is a counter theory with much speculation, each with strengths and weaknesses.

Some even suggest the "sons of God" were dynamic human beings or leaders who were possessed by demons, perhaps from the ungodly line of Lamech. It is certainly true that ungodly people can be possessed by demons, as we see elsewhere in the Bible (e.g., Judas), especially in the Gospels. But demon-possessed people are never called "sons of God," and believers are never said to be capable of being possessed, so even that theory is weak.

When all is said and done, no one can be definitively sure about the Nephilim. Personally, I find the idea that they were gigantic supernatural demigods who were the offspring of demons very unlikely for all the reasons listed above. I also doubt the idea that "sons of God" could be referring to someone who is demon possessed. What this leaves is the idea that the "sons of God" were likely normal human beings who were known to be godly men (likely descendants of Seth but *possibly* from another line), who sinned when they married unbelieving women and produced ungodly, physically strong and violent people who came to be known as the Nephilim, i.e., the "fallen ones" or "giants" (depending on how you translate the Hebrew word *naphal*). This is the view I currently hold, and it was the view of many significant theologians in church history like Augustine, Luther, and Calvin.[5]

The fact is, I am not totally sure. So what this teaches us is that there are times when the Bible presents us with facts and narratives that are hard to interpret and must for the time being remain a mystery to us. Sometimes we do not understand things fully until redemption history progresses. For example, Paul said one mystery that has now been made known was the inclusion of both Jew and Gentiles into one body known as the church (Ephesians 3:1–6; Colossians 1:25–27).

Other things in the Bible remain a mystery, like the exact timing of the second coming. Either way, we must agree that we just do not know everything there is to know about what the Bible reveals, even concerning the past. This does not mean that we cannot know anything for sure, because what the Bible asserts and is clear about should be believed to be true. For as Jesus said, the "word is truth"

(John 17:17). But it does mean that we should be humble when it comes to understanding controversial or ambiguous passages that sound, biblical scholars cannot fully agree on.

There is one thing, however, that should fully be agreed on when it comes to the Nephilim. This was a dark period in human history where sexual sin lent itself to wholesale corruption. The *ESV Study Bible* does an excellent job in its text notes pointing out the similarity of effects between the union of the "sons of God" and the "daughters of man" and the sin that took place at the fall of Adam and Eve in the garden of Eden, and perhaps this is why this text is in the Bible—to warn us of sin and its pattern (see also James 1:14–15). It is on this note that we will close.

> Though it would be difficult to determine which of these three views may be correct, it is clear that the kind of relationship described here involved some form of grievous sexual perversion, wherein the "sons of God" saw and with impunity took any women ("daughters of man") that they wanted. The sequence here in Genesis 6:2 ("saw . . . attractive [good] . . . took") parallels the sequence of the fall in 3:6 ("saw . . . good . . . took"). In both cases, something good in God's creation is used in disobedience and sinful rebellion against God, with tragic consequences.[6]

As Paul said, these kinds of stories serve as a warning to not make the same kinds of mistakes (1 Corinthians 10:11). We, as God's people, should not be unequally yoked with an unbeliever (2 Corinthians 6:14–7:1), for the compromise of righteousness mixed with unrighteousness will only lead to corruption.

15

"No One Knows the Day or the Hour"

≡ MATTHEW 24:36 ≡

I t has been the belief throughout all of Christian history that Jesus is both fully God and fully man. This was the teaching the apostles passed on to the church through the New Testament. When these ideas were attacked by false teachers, mystics, and philosophers, the church was forced to articulate, crystallize, and formalize the official orthodox teaching of God's Word concerning the matter.[1]

The church councils at Nicea (325 AD), Constantinople (381 AD), and Chalcedon (451 AD) all helped to solidify the church's understanding of the two natures of Christ. The idea of a church council to articulate and clarify the church's essential doctrinal beliefs draws its origins back to the book of Acts, where in chapter 15 the apostles met to discuss whether it was necessary for new believers to be circumcised according to the Law of Moses (their conclusion was no, since we are not under the Mosaic law code anymore since it was fulfilled by Christ).

Early church theologians like Irenaeus (130–202 AD) and Hippolytus (170–235 AD) were some of the first to clarify the doctrinal teachings about Christ in things like a "statement of faith" or a "baptismal affirmation" (beliefs that one would affirm at their baptism). Soon the church would formulate "creeds" (from the Latin word *credo* meaning "I believe") that would articulate the essentials of Christian teaching about Jesus and other such essentials in the Apostles' Creed and the Nicene Creed.

All of what we believe about Jesus had to be rightly derived from Scripture in its original context. In his doctrinal masterpiece to the church, the apostle Paul in Romans began his letter with these theologically rich words:

> Paul, a servant of Christ Jesus, called as an apostle and set apart for the gospel of God—which he promised beforehand through his prophets in the Holy Scriptures—concerning his Son, Jesus Christ *our Lord, who was a descendant of David according to the flesh and was appointed to be the powerful Son of God* according to the Spirit of holiness by the resurrection of the dead.
>
> Romans 1:1–4, emphasis mine

Here Paul calls Jesus "Lord" (a title of divinity) while also saying that he was a human descendant of David's line, which is what "according to the flesh" communicates. Further, his resurrection from the dead proved that he was the "powerful Son of God" (one who is in essence God) and serves as the evidence that this "once dead but now alive man" is none other than the living God in human flesh.

What this means then is that Jesus possesses all the attributes of humanity and all the attributes of divinity and as such is the only one qualified to be the mediator between humankind and God (1 Timothy 2:5). As God, then, he would naturally possess the ability to "know all things," also known as *omniscience*. He clearly demonstrated that quality in his life and ministry when he knew things that any normal human could not possibly have known. The disciples affirmed it (John 16:30), and even Peter would say to him, "Lord, you know all things" (John 21:17).

He knew the thoughts of people (Matthew 12:25; Mark 2:8; Luke 6:8; John 2:25), he knew where Nathaniel was sitting before he even met him (John 1:48), and he knew who it was that did not believe in him (John 6:64). One time he told Peter to go to the lake, cast out his line, and in the mouth of the first fish he caught there would be a coin that would pay for both Jesus' and Peter's temple tax. You've heard of the facetious "money trees," but how about "money fish"? I wish I had a pond full of that kind of fish. But seriously, how did he know there would be a coin in a "random" fish's mouth? Simple. He was God, and God knows all things. Plus, it was likely another one of his miracles.

Yet, in Matthew 24:36 (and repeated in Mark 13:32), Jesus makes a stunning statement:

> "Now concerning that day and hour no one knows—neither the angels of heaven nor the Son—except the Father alone."

How could he say that he did not know the day or the hour of his second coming if he was truly God? Theologians for centuries have been able to reconcile this by understanding that as both man and God, Jesus had two natures—a human nature and a divine nature. This means that he had two minds (two centers of consciousness) and two wills (seen clearly in his agony in the garden of Gethsemane—Matthew 26:39).

This does not mean that he was two separate people, or that he had a multiple personality. It simply means there were times "as a man" he chose to access his "divine mind" that knew all things, and there were times when he chose not to. Apparently, on this particular issue (the second coming), he chose not to access his "divine mind" so as to leave it a mystery to be revealed during the future church age. Can you imagine how it would change us if we knew when that day would come?

Jesus purposefully "limited himself" on certain divine attributes during the time of his earthly ministry. One might surmise that simply taking on "human form" would put limits on him to a certain degree (like omnipresence).[2] It was not necessary to access all those privileges in keeping with his current mission on earth. Paul would echo that sentiment in Philippians 2, when he would write that Jesus

> who, though he was in the form of God, did not count equality with God a thing to be grasped [or "taken advantage of" or "held onto"], but emptied himself, by taking the form of a servant, being born in the likeness of men. And being found in human form, he humbled himself by becoming obedient to the point of death, even death on a cross.
>
> Philippians 2:6–8 ESV

Paul's holding up the humility of Christ here is an example for us. Even though Jesus was God in the flesh, he chose, while he was here on earth, not to take full advantage of his divine status, rights, and privileges. Without ceasing to be God, he was still willing to give up certain privileges during the course of his incarnate ministry on earth. This explains why Jesus said what he said earlier in Matthew 24 (and Mark 13). Jesus chose not to access that information. Theologian Wayne Grudem suggests, "This ignorance of the time of his return was true of Jesus' human nature and human consciousness only, for in his divine nature he was certainly omniscient and certainly knew the time when he would return to earth."[3]

It seems to us that he merely chose *at that particular time* (during his earthly ministry) not to access that privileged information.

To some degree, how all of this worked in the life of Jesus is still a big mystery to us, but it's not impossible. The testimony of Scripture is that Jesus *as a human* could still grow, learn, and mature in "wisdom and stature" (Luke 2:52) in his *human mind*, and yet *as God* he could "know all things" (John 21:17) in his *divine mind*.

Jesus said that only the "Father" *at that time* knew the timing of his return. But surely Jesus as the resurrected, glorified, and ascended Son of God now knows what the perfect timing is, as he certainly chose to access his divine mind on the matter as Revelation 22:20 suggests: "Surely I am coming soon" (ESV).

Jesus is a perplexing and yet glorious figure. Certain things about him will always remain a mystery to us because of our finite minds and limited understanding. Yet there are many other things that we *do know* for sure about him. He is God in the flesh. Fully God, fully man. Eternal. Savior. Lord. Sovereign over all, and coming King! Let us live as if his coming is going to happen today.

16

A Nose Full of Quail

One of the most humorous chapters in the Bible has to be the Old Testament book of Numbers, chapter 11. In one sense it is sad, because it is a rather unflattering and embarrassing moment for the people of God who are doing what they should not: complaining. However, when you look at the exasperated responses of Moses, and God's almost comical solution to the matter, it is hard not to chuckle.

Slightly over a year had gone by since the Israelites left Egypt, miraculously delivered from the plagues by the LORD and having witnessed the incredible parting of the Red Sea. The LORD made a covenant with them at Mount Sinai, and the debacle of idolatry that happened at the bottom of the mountain there was over. Obedience was reestablished among them, and it was time to move on from the wilderness of Sinai toward the Promised Land. With the tabernacle in hand, the ark of the covenant before them, and the "cloud of the LORD" over them, they pressed on.

On their way, like on a typical road trip, the people start to grumble and complain. The text simply says they were complaining about their "misfortunes" or "hardship" (Numbers 11:1), so we do not know the real reason for this initial gripe. But it's loud, and the LORD hears it, and he's angry about it to the point where he unloads judgment right away. The fire of God consumes the outskirts of the camp, and interestingly, the people cry out to Moses (instead of the LORD). Moses intercedes for them, and the fire dies out.[1] Did they learn their lesson? Hardly. It's going to get worse.

Among the people were a small group of non-Israelites, and soon after the previous complaining subsided, a new complaint emerged. The Bible says "the riffraff" (or "rabble") among them had a strong craving for other food (Numbers 11:4). Once again, a spirit of discontent spreads throughout the camp; the Israelites jump on board and the complaints ring out all over again:

> Who will feed us meat? We remember the free fish we ate in Egypt, along with cucumbers, melons, leeks, onions, and garlic. But now our appetite is gone; there is nothing to look at but this manna!
>
> Numbers 11:4–6

Apparently, the steady diet of manna cakes and manna muffins was not quite satisfying, and they longed to go back to the flavorful food of their slave years. Yes, you read that right—they would exchange their freedom for food. In the meantime, they could never really figure out what the manna was to begin with. In fact, the word *manna* literally means "what is it?"

The Bible goes on to say that manna resembled something like coriander seed that had resin-like qualities to it that could be boiled and shaped into cakes—tasting somewhat like a pastry. The manna would show up along with the dew on the ground and be harvested every morning (except on the Sabbath).

But they were sick of it, and whole families are whining and weeping at the entrance of their tents. And once again, the LORD hears it and he's not happy. After all he's done to deliver them from the most wicked and oppressive bondage, here they are fussing over his miraculous provision because it does not meet their expectations.

God is angry, Moses is perturbed, and one of the most poignant rants you will ever hear in the Bible comes out of Moses' mouth.

> So Moses asked the LORD, "Why have you brought such trouble on your servant? Why are you angry with me, and why do you burden me with all these people? Did I conceive all these people? Did I give them birth so you should tell me, 'Carry them at your breast, as a nanny carries a baby,' to the land that you swore to give their fathers? Where can I get meat to give all these people? For they are weeping to me, 'Give us meat to eat!' I can't carry all these people by myself. They are too much for me. If you are going to treat me like this, please kill me right now if I have found favor with you, and don't let me see my misery anymore."
>
> Numbers 11:11–15

Again, it is both humorous and sad at the same time. Moses essentially says, "Why me? Why have you burdened me with this overwhelming responsibility? I'm not their mom. They whine and moan because they want meat. How am I going to get them meat? I can't do it. I've had enough. These are your people, and if this is the plan you have for me, to continue to lead this fussy people, just kill me now."[2]

Those are the words of an exhausted and exasperated leader, one who has carried the weight on his shoulders and listened to the complaints of tens of thousands of people for a long time. Mercifully, God hears and responds and appoints seventy wise and discerning elders among them to assist Moses. But the LORD is not done. He's still upset at the attitude of his people, and he tells Moses to tell the people to get ready, because meat is coming—in fact, more meat than they will ever want.

> You will eat, not for one day, or two days, or five days, or ten days, or twenty days, but for a whole month—until it comes out of your

nostrils and becomes nauseating to you—because you have rejected the LORD who is among you, and wept before him: "Why did we ever leave Egypt?"

Numbers 11:19–20

Can you hear the LORD's frustration? Believe me when I say there is just as much or more grace and patience in the Old Testament as there is in the New Testament.

What is this meat going to be? We find out soon that it is birds—quail, to be exact (see. v. 31). Sure, it might be nice to have a change for a couple of days, but by the time you have had it constantly for a month, it starts to become nasty. In fact, the LORD says it is going to come out of their noses and nauseate them.

> While the meat was still between their teeth, before it was chewed, the LORD's anger burned against the people, and the LORD struck them with a very severe plague. So they named that place Kibroth-hattaavah, because there they buried the people who had craved the meat.

They did not all die, but many did, and so they named the place Kibroth-hattavah, which is Hebrew for "the graves of the craving." We are unsure what kind of plague hit the guilty ones, and the word translated "chewed" above could also be translated as "exhausted," giving the idea that while they were eating and before the food was gone or "exhausted," they were struck with some kind of food poisoning.[3]

Why is this in the Bible? Again, it's history. It's real, and it happened, and this is clearly a historical account. But theologically, this reminds us again of the LORD exercising his right as a holy God to bring judgment whenever he chooses, and in this instance for people who longed to go back to bondage, who did nothing but complain even after having seen all the miracles the LORD had done for them.

It is as if they were rejecting their deliverance, rejecting the LORD's kindness and provision, and rejecting the Lord himself along with

Moses, their appointed leader. This apparently was enough for the LORD to take action on those who were leading the rebellion.

Finally, the apostle Paul says something about complaining that we would do well to prayerfully consider.

> Do everything without grumbling and arguing, so that you may be blameless and pure, children of God who are faultless in a crooked and perverted generation, among whom you shine like stars in the world, by holding firm to the word of life.
>
> Philippians 2:14–16

Are we people of grace who are thankful for his grace? Are we displaying humility and gratitude for all that we have been given? Or are we rejecting God and his provision through our attitudes of discontent?

All I know is that all we own or possess ultimately comes from God. There are millions of people throughout the world who are starving today, so for whatever manna comes our way today, let's be grateful.

17

Solomon's Many Wives

1 KINGS 11:1–13

You know it's only a matter of time before someone looks at the Bible and says, "See, even God's chosen king had multiple wives and concubines . . . so what's the problem?" With the direction our culture is headed and with the definition of marriage in complete disarray, it will not be a surprise to see some appealing to the Bible (even out of context) in order to justify the appetites of the sexual revolution.

But an important principle needs to be understood. There is a difference between the Bible recording and *describing* the sins of God's people versus *prescribing* their behavior and endorsing it as legitimate in God's eyes. In other words, there is a difference between the *descriptive* and *prescriptive*. The descriptive is simply telling you what happened; the prescriptive is more of a command on how to live to please God.

When it comes to Solomon's life and the lives of many other patriarchs or kings in the Old Testament, we have descriptive behavior, not prescriptive.

From the very beginning of Genesis, we have God's definition of marriage, something that he himself created and instituted to bring him glory. God created Eve as a suitable helper for Adam (Genesis 2:18), and then he "presented her to the man" (Genesis 2:22), which is why in our wedding ceremonies it is tradition for the father to present the bride to her husband. Then Moses tells us,

> This is why a man leaves his father and mother and bonds with his wife, and they become one flesh.
>
> Genesis 2:24

The idea of "one flesh" pictures a covenant unity that is designed to be unbreakable, and it encompasses the relational, emotional, physical, and spiritual bond that God has designed for marriage. Jesus reiterated this truth in Matthew 19:4–6 and Mark 10:5–9. The sanctity and definition of marriage as one man and one woman in a covenant relationship that is designed to last a lifetime exists in both the Old and New Testaments.[1] It is prescriptive in nature, or it is the way God has prescribed and designed it to be.

When we read in the Bible that people like Jacob, David, Solomon, and many others had multiple wives, what we are seeing is a corruption of God's design and plan for marriage. Notice above in Genesis 2:24 that the reference to "wife" is singular, not plural. So when Lamech, the first polygamist in the Bible (Genesis 4:19), took two wives, he was sinning against God's moral will when it comes to marriage.

God would remind us of the potential damage and destruction that would come from having multiple wives when he prophesied through Moses, who when talking about the future kings that Israel would one day have, stated that the king "must not acquire many wives for himself so that his heart won't go astray" (Deuteronomy 17:17).

Tragically, this prophetic warning was not heeded, and the sin of polygamy became common in the ancient world, especially among the kings of Israel. David was known to have at least eight wives (maybe more, see 2 Samuel 5:13), and then we read with horror about David's son Solomon.

> King Solomon loved many foreign women in addition to Pharaoh's daughter: Moabite, Ammonite, Edomite, Sidonian, and Hittite women from the nations about which the LORD had told the Israelites, "You must not intermarry with them, and they must not intermarry with you, because they will turn your heart away to follow their gods." To these women Solomon was deeply attached in love. He had seven hundred wives who were princesses and three hundred who were concubines, and they turned his heart away.
>
> When Solomon was old, his wives turned his heart away to follow other gods. He was not wholeheartedly devoted to the LORD his God, as his father David had been. Solomon followed Ashtoreth, the goddess of the Sidonians, and Milcom, the abhorrent idol of the Ammonites. Solomon did what was evil in the LORD's sight, and unlike his father David, he did not remain loyal to the LORD.
>
> 1 Kings 11:1–6

Several things are incredulous about this account. First, the fact that Solomon had seven hundred wives and three hundred concubines is most disturbing. One has to wonder if he sets the all-time record for polygamous and promiscuous relationships. How could he even begin to have any meaningful relationships with these women? The text says he was "deeply attached to these women in love" (v. 2), but it is likely that he was in love with the sensuality and sexual promiscuity that had captured his heart. He was in love with his sin.[2]

Further, it was a common practice in the ancient Near East to ratify treaties with foreign nations by marrying the king's daughter of another monarchy. This practice was common in modern-day Europe as well during the age of the monarchies like Britain, France, Spain, etc. They did not often marry for love, but for political reasons. For King Solomon, the more wives one had, the more power, influence, and prestige he possessed as a ruler (in the eyes of man).

But all of this violated Moses' prohibition in Deuteronomy 17:17, and in violating the statutes of God, he nullified the conditional agreement that was made with God. For example, in 1 Kings 9 we read:

> As for you, if you walk before me as your father David walked, with a heart of integrity and in what is right, doing everything I have commanded you, and if you keep my statutes and ordinances, I will establish your royal throne over Israel forever, as I promised your father David: You will never fail to have a man on the throne of Israel.
>
> If you or your sons turn away from following me and do not keep my commands—my statutes that I have set before you—and if you go and serve other gods and bow in worship to them, I will cut off Israel from the land I gave them, and I will reject the temple I have sanctified for my name. Israel will become an object of scorn and ridicule among all the peoples.
>
> 1 Kings 9:4–7

Solomon had some amazing promises from God, but they were conditional, based on his obedience. He did not need to marry outside of Israel. He did not need to secure alliances with other nations. God promised to establish his throne and bring abundant blessing. But pride goes before a fall, and Solomon, the wisest and wealthiest man in all of Israel, fell far and fell hard.

This is a valuable lesson for all of us. *Blessing follows obedience*, but the path to destruction is paved with sinful choices that follow the "desires of the flesh and the desires of the eyes and the pride of life" (1 John 2:16 ESV).

Solomon's story ended up being a tragic one. His brazen choice to violate the Lord's clearly revealed moral will cost him dearly. Judgment came. The kingdom was ripped in half. His heirs acted foolishly, and idolatry was rampant. The northern ten tribes of Israel were utterly destroyed by their enemies, and only a few kings in the kingdom of Judah to the south did what was right in the Lord's eyes. Eventually, even the Southern Kingdom was exiled to Babylon as a result of their idolatry and shameful sins.

This is not the legacy any man would wish to have—a man who lost his integrity, compromised his principles, abandoned his commitments to God, and followed his flesh. As one scholar put it, "These twin desires for prestige and sensuality led to his nation's downfall."[3] His heart was led astray because Moses' warning went unheeded.

History has proven over and over that when one follows God's plan, there is blessing, but when the moral will of God is purposefully and willfully usurped, it is a recipe for disaster. Such was the case for King Solomon. The irony is that the wisest man who ever lived acted foolishly. This is yet another reminder of how helpless and powerless we are to overcome our sin nature apart from the grace of God. Oh, how we need him.

18

Destroying the Soul and Body in Hell

≡ MATTHEW 10:28 ≡

If God is everywhere (omnipresent), then is God in hell?[1] Most people have never considered that question, and many assume that hell by definition is not only a place of punishment, but a "banishment from the presence of God."[2] After all, in the parable of the sheep and the goats told by Jesus in Matthew 25, when Christ returns at his second coming to judge the earth, the evildoers who are alive at that time will be judged and sent to hell, and the Lord will say, "Depart from me, you who are cursed, into the eternal fire prepared for the devil and his angels!" (Matthew 25:41).

So if they are told to "depart" from him, doesn't that mean that where they go, God is not present? *Not necessarily*. This is because if God is omnipresent and fills the universe (cf. Jeremiah 23:23–24), he must be there in *some sense*. He must certainly be there to *sustain* its very existence, because Hebrews tells us that the Son of God is "sustaining all things by his powerful word"

(Hebrews 1:3). This means the universe (both seen and unseen) would cease to exist or would implode if it wasn't for the power of God to sustain it. Indeed, Paul tells us that "by him all things hold together" (Colossians 1:7).

Further, he would also have to be there in another sense in order to execute his judgment for all eternity, for the Scriptures clearly teach that hell is a place of God's wrath, where *God is present to punish* all that is wicked "forever and ever" (Revelation 14:11; 20:10), i.e., an *eternal punishment* (Matthew 25:46).[3] Though hell as a place of *eternal conscious punishment* is a revulsive thought to us, it is nevertheless a necessary biblical doctrine to hold as the Bible clearly teaches that God will punish the wicked for all eternity. I would suggest that we are not capable of fully understanding how awful our sin actually is before an eternally holy God, and thus his punishment and wrath are never disproportionate. He would not be a God of love or a God of justice if he chose not to punish evil.

But then, where does this leave us? In what sense are people "departing" (Matthew 25:41) from Christ for all eternity if he is still there in hell to *sustain* and *punish*? Theologian Wayne Grudem provides us with a helpful solution when he suggests that "God is present in different ways in different places, or that God acts differently in different places in his creation."[4] He is present in hell to sustain and punish, but he is not there to bless. "In fact, most of the time that the Bible talks about God's presence, it is referring to God's presence to bless."[5] But in hell, the activity of blessing that often comes with God's presence is missing.

So in that sense, when Christ instructs the wicked to depart from him, he is essentially condemning them to an eternal existence in hell that is absent of his presence to bless them in any sense. There is no grace, no forgiveness, and no ability to enjoy life in any way. It is a dreadful thought, and one that ought to motivate us to share our faith so as to "win as many as possible" (1 Corinthians 9:19).

Knowing that God is in hell in the sense of *sustaining* and *punishing* also helps us interpret something that Christ said to his disciples during the season of ministry where he sent them out two by two to preach the good news of the kingdom. In Matthew 10, Jesus summons his twelve disciples and decides to give them some hands-on training and experience, giving them authority over unclean spirits as well as the ability to drive out disease and sickness. They were to preach that the "the kingdom of heaven is near" (Matthew 10:7), authenticating Jesus as the Messiah and they, as his apostles, his messengers.

He gave them a series of instructions on what to do and what not to do, and then warned them of the dangers that they might encounter along the way. Though they would have God's empowering presence with them, they would still face persecution, both in their current mission and even long after Christ ascended back to heaven. Suffering would come, but this was to be expected, because "a disciple is not above his teacher, or a slave above his master" (Matthew 10:24). If they persecuted and hated Christ, then the disciples should expect to be persecuted and hated as well since they were Christ's ambassadors and messengers.

But he tells them not to be afraid of this. God will one day correct and avenge all injustices. He will make right all wrongs and will set them in their proper place. And in saying this, he was meaning to instill confidence and courage in these men. Then he reminds them of who it is that has the power over their body and soul, namely Jesus. And he says this in a peculiar way.

> Don't fear those who kill the body but are not able to kill the soul; rather, fear him who is able to destroy both soul and body in hell. Aren't two sparrows sold for a penny? Yet not one of them falls to the ground without your Father's consent. But even the hairs of your head have all been counted. So don't be afraid; you are worth more than many sparrows.
>
> Matthew 10:28–31

Jesus told them not to be afraid of those who only have the power to kill the body (their persecutors in this life); rather, they should have a healthy reverence for the one who is able to destroy the soul and body in hell (Jesus). In other words, don't be afraid of man—they can only kill your body, a body that was not meant to live forever anyway. Rather, you should fear and revere God, who has the power not only over your body, but your soul as well, and you know that both are equally in his powerfully sovereign hands.

Now, most people might think that when he was referring to the one who "is able to destroy both soul and body in hell," he was referring to Satan. But that is not the case. Based on what we learned above, the person who has the authority over souls in hell is none other than God himself, who is there to sustain and punish the wicked for all eternity.

And since hell is an eternal punishment, we know that to "destroy" does not mean annihilate; rather, it means to "suffer great loss or harm." God's wrath is powerful and has destructive effects, but it does not cause a person to cease to exist. You can have either eternal life in heaven or eternal death in hell. And God is the one who sends people to hell, and he is the one who sustains and governs hell and all that happens there.

So we must not think that Jesus is saying that the disciples should be afraid of Satan, who has some supposed power to destroy both soul and body in hell. Rather, he is telling them not to be afraid of evil—for all evil can do is take away the body—but only God has the power over both body *and* soul.

In fact, I would assert to you that the modern-day conception of Satan being the one who sends people to hell and punishes them there is not even true. That is actually God's job. Satan is one day bound to go there himself for punishment for all eternity. As we observed above, Jesus will one day send the wicked along with the devil and his angels into a place of final judgment called the "lake of fire," an eternal hell and place of torment. John tells us in Revelation that it is a "lake of fire and sulfur" where torment will take place "day and night forever and ever" (Revelation 20:10).

But until that day comes, Satan is allowed to roam free about heaven and earth (Job 1:6–7); is known as the "ruler of this world"

(John 12:31; 14:30; 16:11)—meaning the evil world system that exists; and is active in opposing God and his servants as an adversary (though he is limited by God's sovereign power). He is not yet confined to hell, nor is he ruling in hell. He will one day end up there, but not before the appointed time.

Sometimes I think we give Satan way too much credit and ascribe him way too much power than he actually has. To be sure, he is the chief opponent of God, is a created being with supernatural power, the originator of sin, and seeks to oppose and destroy all that is from God, but he is still subservient to God's control and power.

He is not always the one to blame for our sin. When we say, "the devil made me do it," we cannot use that as an excuse to dismiss ourselves from our own wickedness that is naturally in our hearts. Sure, he tempts us. He most definitely is responsible for much of the evil in this world. But we cannot overlook and explain away the problems that arise and the evil that exists that finds its roots in the heart of man.

Satan is a bad dude. But apart from Christ, we are too. Unbelievers are held captive by their sin and are enslaved by Satan's power, but his power is no match for the power of God, which comes to us through the gospel—the power that wrestles us away from the chains of sin and death so that we can be set free to experience the life that is truly life (1 Timothy 6:19).

19

Herod Eaten by Worms

≡ ACTS 12:20–24 ≡

Idolatry is perhaps one of the worst sins, if not *the* worst sin. Idolatry is "paying divine honor to any created thing."[1] Throughout the Bible, humanity has struggled with this sin since the original fall in the garden of Eden, being tempted to "be like God" (Genesis 3:5). Our tendency to compete with God or to ascribe godhood to things that are not gods pervades our existence. Therefore the LORD began his list of Ten Commandments with the prohibition of having any so-called gods before him or worshiping any created image (Exodus 20:1–6).

Whether it be worshiping inanimate objects made of wood or stone, or things like animals, celestial objects, electronics, sex, money, status, or even ourselves, anything that competes with God for our mind's attention and heart's affection can rightly be called an idol. As those created in his image, we are made for his glory (Isaiah 43:7) and are commanded to love him with all our "heart, soul, mind, and strength" (Mark 12:30).

When Herod Agrippa I (grandson of Herod the Great) accepted the praise of men who were saying he was like a god, the one true God exercised his right to bring judgment in rather dramatic fashion.

The context of this is found in Acts 12. The book of Acts traces the birth of the church and the spread of the gospel from its earliest stages, highlighting both the ministries of the apostle Peter and the apostle Paul. As the church grew, persecution began to grow, especially from the unbelieving Jews who were antagonistic to this new sect of Christ-followers who claimed Jesus was Israel's Messiah.

Herod Agrippa I was the king in northern Palestine from 37–44 AD. Prior to his reign, he was one of many princes who had been born out of the Herodian dynasty. He had a reputation of being an eloquent man who struggled greatly with self-love and vanity (as most of the Herods did). He was a master of politics, a keen diplomat who knew how to schmooze his way into good relationships with both the new emperor Claudius at Rome and the Jews of his ever-expanding region of rule in Palestine.

As a non-Jew himself (he was Idumaean, from Edomite origin), he knew that in order to find favor with the Jews he reigned over, he would have to seek to identify with many of their causes. Chief among them at the time was the persecution of Christians, and Acts 12 teaches us that Herod "laid hands on" or seized many followers of Christ, mistreating them and even executing the apostle James (the brother of the apostle John). He also had Peter arrested, since all of this seemed to please the Jews, but Peter miraculously escaped prison through angelic intervention.

Following his escape, Herod had the guards executed and traveled off to Caesarea Maritime on the Mediterranean Sea, where he enjoyed time at his luxurious palace with amazing views of the ocean and fresh water piped in via aqueduct from the nearby mountains of Mount Carmel.

According to Acts 12, a trade dispute had surfaced with two Phoenician cities, Tyre and Sidon. Herod, in his anger, had put a blockade or embargo in place that apparently was crippling these two cities, and they desired to bring peace to the situation right away. In their desperate attempt to fix things, the people (or some representatives) of these cities somehow had won over a key official of Herod's palace to their cause. Negotiations took place, an agreement was made, and Herod made a great speech in the large amphitheater (which was recently excavated and can be visited today).[2]

Luke tells us that Herod sat on his throne in "royal robes" (Acts 12:21), and the ancient Jewish historian Josephus says that Herod put on a garment made of silver that sparkled in the early morning sunlight. Though we do not have the content of his speech, the beauty of the moment and the elation of the people caused them to say, "It's the voice of a god and not of a man!"[3]

Such flattery was apparently effective because Herod did not seem to correct them, perhaps enjoying the moment and basking in the early morning sun. Luke tells us what happens next.

> At once an angel of the Lord struck him because he did not give the glory to God, and he was eaten by worms and died.
>
> Acts 12:23

Instant judgment. The unrebuked, "impious flattery" (see Josephus, *Antiquities* 19.8.2) of the people was his "downfall."[4] He relished it, and God sent an angel to inflict punishment. According to Josephus, the painful affliction lasted for five days before Herod died an excruciating and violent death at the age of fifty-four. Luke tells us the cause of death was from being eaten by worms, an internal nightmare to be sure.

The irony is that he was consumed from the inside—and sin, our greatest disease, is a lot like that. The only cure for it is the gospel, the very thing that Herod was seeking to wipe out. But this narrative account is not merely showing us God's creative methods in exacting judgment.

Rather, Luke's purpose is undoubtedly to give a historical account of the opposition to the gospel and the suffering its messengers faced.

Here in Acts 12 we see James martyred and Peter imprisoned. But even so, the gospel remains unchained. It will not be stopped. Bock suggests that the message of contrast is on full display.

> In sum, an opponent of the gospel is judged while Peter is freed. Mercy and judgment appear side by side. God is active on behalf of the church. We see a contrast between those God protects and those he judges. Peter is protected at this point by a deliverance even the disciples find hard to believe, whereas Herod is struck down for opposing the people of God and for his arrogance in allowing himself to be declared equal to God. And yet James is not delivered but suffers a martyr's death. . . . This points to how God works in different ways with different people. As the church expands, the persecution continues with differing consequences for the church's members.[5]

The story line of Acts shows us the power of the ever-spreading gospel and the natural opposition of sinful humanity toward it. But no matter how much suffering God's people have to endure, the God of the universe who stands as judge will have the final say. In many ways, Herod's demise echoes the words of the Lord spoken through the prophet Isaiah:

> I am the Lord. That is my name, and I will not give my glory to another or my praise to idols.
>
> Isaiah 42:8

This will surely be true in a fully visible sense at the end of this present age when the Lord returns in judgment, but in Acts 12, some of that prophetic truth came full force through an angel sent to defend the Lord's honor at a critical time in the life of the church. In the words of the famous "Battle Hymn of the Republic": "His truth is marching on."

20

Send the Choir into Battle First

A s the American church has changed over the last fifty years, the use of church choirs to assist in leading worship has waned. For some, this is a great tragedy. Others feel differently, seeing them as outdated and unnecessary. Many churches have replaced choirs with stimulating audio and visual technology that attempts to create an experiential atmosphere to connect with God. It is possible that some churches have both (i.e., Brooklyn Tabernacle), but most churches do not have the resources for this.

Personally, I love a good choir, and I believe that if a church has the resources to do it, it should be taken advantage of. Many people in our churches (not just the praise team) have beautiful voices and love using their gifts in worship to God. Further, the fellowship that a choir experiences as they practice and perform together is yet another way the church is strengthened in its relationships, using a shared experience to grow spiritually together as they serve the body of Christ.

One thing abundantly true throughout biblical history is that God's people have always been drawn to music, and the book of Psalms is a sure testimony to that. Many psalms were sung by God's people as they pilgrimaged to Jerusalem, and were included in temple worship by some of the Levites (1 Chronicles 15:16). Coronations, feasts, festivals, and celebrations of victory in battle were often times when music was incorporated into the community life of Israel.

Jesus and his disciples sang a hymn at the Last Supper (Matthew 26:30), and Paul gave instructions to the church with regard to music as they sang psalms, hymns, and spiritual songs to each other with gratitude in their hearts (Colossians 3:16). Music is the expression of the heart toward a loving and grace-giving God, and will accompany us into eternity as we sing new songs to the Lord our God (Revelation 5:8; 14:3).

Yet there is one particular story in the Old Testament that surprises us when it comes to utilizing music. It is true that music was employed upon return from battle to celebrate victory (1 Samuel 18:6–7), but what if I told you that at one point the LORD decided to have a choir lead the army in joyful song on their way to the battlefield, as if they were proclaiming victory even before the battle started?

That is what happened in 2 Chronicles 20, as one of the good kings of the southern Israelite nation of Judah commanded the army to lead the way as they headed into a battle.

After King David had died in Israel, his son Solomon reigned. Solomon, as we know, was a wise king who amassed great wealth and power. He built and dedicated the temple for Israel. But Solomon had some major sin issues. He had hundreds of wives and concubines, and he intermarried with pagan women who led his heart astray from God. Though he returned to God in the end, the damage had been done.

As a result of his disobedience, God disciplined Solomon by promising to divide the kingdom of Israel into two parts after his death—there was a political kingdom in the north that kept the name *Israel*, and there was a political kingdom in the south that was named the kingdom of *Judah*. Both kingdoms were composed of Israelites—they just had different political names.

As you read Old Testament history, you will discover that all the kings who ruled in the Northern Kingdom were corrupt. Eventually these tribes were dispersed and destroyed by pagan nations (mostly Assyria). Not even *one* of Israel's kings could be labeled good because they refused to follow the Lord.

However, there were a few kings who ruled the Southern Kingdom who did follow in the ways of the Lord. King Jehoshaphat was one of those kings. Jehoshaphat, known as a king of great wealth and honor, was a king who had initiated spiritual reform among his people. He tore down the pagan idols that had been set up within his kingdom and commanded the Levites to go out and teach people the Scriptures.

Spiritually he is described as a man who was devoted to the Lord, and he was blessed. He had made some mistakes in his early years, but overall he was a good king, establishing justice in the land. But he would be tested. In 2 Chronicles 20, we see one of his greatest moments.

> After this, the Moabites and Ammonites, together with some of the Meunites, came to fight against Jehoshaphat. People came and told Jehoshaphat, "A vast number from beyond the Dead Sea and from Edom has come to fight against you; they are already in Hazazon-tamar" (that is, En-gedi). Jehoshaphat was afraid, and he resolved to seek the Lord.[1] Then he proclaimed a fast for all Judah, who gathered to seek the Lord. They even came from all the cities of Judah to seek him.
>
> 2 Chronicles 20:1–4

Notice what Jehoshaphat didn't do. He didn't start complaining or blame anyone because trouble arrived at his doorstep. He didn't get angry, mad, or curse. Nor did he run to look for wise counsel among his military commanders.

The very first thing Jehoshaphat did was to call a fast and go immediately to prayer. It was his natural response. He knew he was in trouble. He was outnumbered, for sure. He was facing death and defeat for him and all his people. Surrender probably would not have mattered, because they would have probably been put to death anyway. This was a desperate moment, and the most powerful weapon in the king's arsenal was prayer.

> Then Jehoshaphat stood in the assembly of Judah and Jerusalem in the Lord's temple before the new courtyard. He said: LORD, God of our ancestors, are you not the God who is in heaven, and do you not rule over all the kingdoms of the nations? Power and might are in your hand, and no one can stand against you. Are you not our God who drove out the inhabitants of this land before your people Israel and who gave it forever to the descendants of Abraham your friend?
>
> 2 Chronicles 20:5–7

Notice the king begins with worship. He worships God for who he is, in all of his power and might, in all of his glory. He comes into God's presence and acknowledges God's rightful place and reign over them, almost as if saying, *"Hallowed be thy name."* Then he remembers God's faithfulness in Israel's past, recounting their victories under Joshua as they possessed the land.

This is a powerful reminder to worship the LORD even in a crisis, to recognize his character and sovereign power over every circumstance we are in. In fact, God may have purposefully put us in that circumstance. Surely that's what happened here. The LORD put them in this circumstance *so that his solution to it would bring him ultimate glory.* And after giving glory to God and appealing to his faithfulness in the past, King Jehoshaphat claims the promises of God.

> They have lived in the land and have built you a sanctuary in it for your name and have said, "If disaster comes on us—sword or judgment, pestilence or famine—we will stand before this temple and before you, for your name is in this temple. We will cry out to you because of our distress, and you will hear and deliver."
>
> 1 Chronicles 20:8–9

In any crisis the believer should look for the promises of God. They are there as reminders in order to strengthen our trust in the God who has proven himself worthy of our faith. We find these promises in God's Word, and so it is helpful to pray the words of Scripture back to God and to reflect on who he is and what he said he will/would do. This is what the king is doing here. Jehoshaphat then admits their powerlessness and great need.

> Now here are the Ammonites, Moabites, and the inhabitants of Mount Seir. You did not let Israel invade them when Israel came out of the land of Egypt, but Israel turned away from them and did not destroy them. Look how they repay us by coming to drive us out of your possession that you gave us as an inheritance. Our God, will you not judge them? For we are powerless before this vast number that comes to fight against us. We do not know what to do, but we look to you.
>
> 1 Chronicles 20:10–12

This is something that all of us, as we stand before God, have to understand: On our own, in our own power and strength, we are powerless and helpless. We cannot save ourselves. We need God to save us. This is especially true when it comes to our sin. We need a Savior. And here in this context, the king models the kind of humility, dependency, and trust that is needed when we are unable to save ourselves from that which is bent on destroying us.

What truly stands out is verse 12. Jehoshaphat is not afraid as the king of Judah to stand up in front of all his people and admit that he does not know what to do when it comes to the approaching enemy. But he does know what to do when that scenario occurs—he looks to the LORD for help. Jehoshaphat is making a stunning profession of faith and trust in the person and power of God.

Look at what the king has done. He has set a clear pattern for us to follow even today.

1. Worship God.
2. Claim his promises.

3. Admit your helplessness and need.

4. Profess your faith and trust.

The LORD's response to all of this is stunning, and is worth the extended read.

> All Judah was standing before the LORD with their dependents, their wives, and their children. In the middle of the congregation, the Spirit of the LORD came on Jahaziel (son of Zechariah, son of Benaiah, son of Jeiel, son of Mattaniah, a Levite from Asaph's descendants), and he said, "Listen carefully, all Judah and you inhabitants of Jerusalem, and King Jehoshaphat. This is what the LORD says: 'Do not be afraid or discouraged because of this vast number, for the battle is not yours, but God's. Tomorrow, go down against them. You will see them coming up the Ascent of Ziz, and you will find them at the end of the valley facing the Wilderness of Jeruel. You do not have to fight this battle. Position yourselves, stand still, and see the salvation of the LORD. He is with you, Judah and Jerusalem. Do not be afraid or discouraged. Tomorrow, go out to face them, for the LORD is with you.'"
>
> 2 Chronicles 20:13–17

What a promise. The LORD raises up a prophet who gives them assurance through the word of the LORD. Not only will the LORD be with them, but they will not even have to fight this battle. All they should do is stand still in faith and watch. Upon hearing this amazing word from God, Jehoshaphat responds.

> Then Jehoshaphat knelt low with his face to the ground, and all Judah and the inhabitants of Jerusalem fell down before the LORD to worship him. Then the Levites from the sons of the Kohathites and the Korahites stood up to praise the LORD God of Israel shouting loudly.
>
> 1 Chronicles 20:18–19

The response to the word from the LORD was continued humility, worship, and praise. They had postured themselves perfectly before the LORD, and his promise of victory gave them all the confidence they needed. In fact, they trusted the LORD so much at this point that they did something very unusual. They put the choir in front of the army. After all, the battle was not theirs but the LORD's.

> In the morning they got up early and went out to the wilderness of Tekoa. As they were about to go out, Jehoshaphat stood and said, "Hear me, Judah and you inhabitants of Jerusalem. Believe in the LORD your God, and you will be established; believe in his prophets, and you will succeed." Then he consulted with the people and appointed some to sing for the LORD and some to praise the splendor of his holiness. When they went out in front of the armed forces, they kept singing:
> Give thanks to the LORD, for his faithful love endures forever.
> The moment they began their shouts and praises, the LORD set an ambush against the Ammonites, Moabites, and the inhabitants of Mount Seir who came to fight against Judah, and they were defeated. The Ammonites and Moabites turned against the inhabitants of Mount Seir and completely annihilated them. When they had finished with the inhabitants of Seir, they helped destroy each other.
>
> 1 Chronicles 20:20–23

What an amazing sight. God's people march into battle. Their leader calls them to trust in God, to believe in his word. They worship as they go—the choir leading the way in song, praising, singing, giving thanks, and remembering God's faithful love. *And as they obeyed*, God intervened on their behalf. He answered their prayers.

> When Judah came to a place overlooking the wilderness, they looked for the large army, but there were only corpses lying on the ground; nobody had escaped.
>
> 1 Chronicles 20:24

There it was. Victory. The LORD's promise was realized, and the king and his people went down to gather the plunder and valuables that the enemy left behind. On the other side of faith and obedience was blessing.

> So they came into Jerusalem to the LORD's temple with harps, lyres, and trumpets. The terror of God was on all the kingdoms of the lands when they heard that the LORD had fought against the enemies of Israel. Then Jehoshaphat's kingdom was quiet, for his God gave him rest on every side.
>
> 1 Chronicles 20:28–30

Worshiping the LORD with continued praise and thanksgiving, King Jehoshaphat and his people returned to Jerusalem victorious and at peace. It was truly nontraditional to have a choir lead them into battle, but in the midst of their circumstances, they recognized that their only hope was to worship God, claim his promises, admit their helplessness and need, and profess their faith and confidence in the Lord.

The same is true for us. As we go into the world where there is much spiritual warfare, we too are to be strong in the LORD and in the power of his might (Ephesians 6:10). We look not to ourselves and our own strength, but to him who will fight our battles on our behalf. We put on the armor of God (Ephesians 6:11–18), equipping ourselves with truth, righteousness, the gospel, faith, the assurance of our salvation, the Word of God, and prayer (all the pieces God intends for us to employ)—and we find ourselves able to stand firm in the heat of battle.

Thankfully, we too have a God who has already gone before us and has defeated our enemy for us at the cross, and the empty tomb reminds us that we have all the spiritual blessings that are found in a victorious Christ. Let us sing, rejoice, and give thanks. For the God who brings us peace reigns over all.

21

Death at Communion

There is no such thing as a perfect church. Nor is there a perfect pastor, or a perfect Christian. Let's face it—nobody is perfect. But this is never an excuse for us to *continue* in sin. Rather, it explains the reason why we *still struggle* with sin. The fact is, Christ died to pay the *penalty* for sin, but until we reach heaven or the Lord comes back (whichever comes first), we will still wage an ongoing battle with the *presence* of sin because we still live in our fallen flesh.[1]

But there's hope. First of all, God's forgiving grace is sufficient to cover all past, present, and future sin. And second, we are not alone in our present battle. Through the indwelling Holy Spirit (Romans 8:13), we can find success in overcoming the *power* of sin that our fallen flesh still struggles with. God has also given us his Word, prayer, and the accountability of the local church to help us grow spiritually while we continue in our commitment to forsake sin. Then we can experience real life.

The church is designed to be a place where the gospel is not only believed, but lived out. The gospel demands that we preach a message of repentance and faith both inside and outside the church. *But what happens when the church loses its mission and sense of purpose and begins to take a flippant attitude toward sin or the message that Christ died to deliver us from it?*

Quick answer: The church begins to die. And in one particular case, this literally became true.

In the New Testament, there is a church where a casual and flippant attitude toward sin was abundantly present—Corinth. Ancient Corinth in Greece was known as a "party city." It was a major thoroughfare for seafaring traffic, and many people frequented the city, especially while its version of the Olympic Games, known as the Isthmian games, was going on. In many ways, it was the Las Vegas of ancient Greece—"sin city." Lots of pagan idolatry, sexual promiscuity, drunkenness, carousing, and general debauchery pervaded the culture there.

So you can imagine what a temptation it was for the brand-new Christians in Corinth who were saved and delivered from those past sins. They still had to battle the flesh and the culture all around them. Many were successful, and many were not. In fact, in 1 Corinthians 5, the church was confronted by the apostle Paul for not dealing with a case of incest (sleeping with a stepmom). Could it get much worse than that? Well, yes.

In 1 Corinthians 11, Paul further confronts the church for not dealing with a very public sin that was happening when the church came together to celebrate the Lord's Supper. In addition to celebrating the bread and the cup, they would also participate in a common meal together, and these times of communion and sharing of a meal became known as *agape* meals or "love feasts" (cf. Jude 12).

But in Corinth, there was not a lot of godly Christian love exhibited at these feasts. Paul's words are worthy of note:

> Now in giving this instruction I do not praise you, since you come together not for the better but for the worse. For to begin with, I

hear that when you come together as a church there are divisions among you, and in part I believe it. Indeed, it is necessary that there be factions among you, so that those who are approved may be recognized among you. When you come together, then, it is not to eat the Lord's Supper. For at the meal, each one eats his own supper. So one person is hungry while another gets drunk! Don't you have homes in which to eat and drink? Or do you despise the church of God and humiliate those who have nothing? What should I say to you? Should I praise you? I do not praise you in this matter!

1 Corinthians 11:17–22

So the fellowship meal and communion service in Corinth was riddled with problems and inappropriate behavior. First, there were divisions among them. Certainly there were personality differences, cliques, and those who separated themselves from others based on allegiances (see 1 Corinthians 1:10–13). But more than that, there were differing socioeconomic ladders. Groups and subgroups existed, and in Greco-Roman culture, there was often a division between the wealthy and the poor.

These differences showed up dramatically at the love feasts. Apparently, some well-to-do Christians had an abundance of food that they were unwilling to share with other believers who were not so well off. More shocking is that some were getting drunk, humiliating both themselves and others while desecrating the unity of the church and shaming the sacred practice of communion. It was so reprehensible that Paul told them that they could not even call it the Lord's Supper.

Not all of them were doing this, which made it easy to see who was sincere about following Christ and his commands and who was not (v. 19). But others were making a mockery of what should have been a demonstration of unity with Christ and one another. The Lord's Supper was meant to be a special time where the church remembered Christ's sacrifice to deliver them from sin (11:25), but instead it became an occasion to revel in sin.

As you can imagine, Paul was quite upset. Not only were they taking the bread and the cup in an "unworthy manner" (11:27), the church as a whole was seemingly doing nothing about it by passively allowing it to continue. As a result, God had apparently decided to take matters into his own hands on such a serious offense. So Paul, in prophetic fashion, announced:

> For whoever eats and drinks without recognizing the body, eats and drinks judgment on himself. This is why many are sick and ill among you, and many have fallen asleep.
>
> 1 Corinthians 11:29–30

Did you see that? Some of these Corinthian Christians had become physically weak and sick, and others had actually died ("fallen asleep" is a euphemism for death) because of their participation in or passive attitude toward this very serious public sin. God personally stepped in and brought forth a chastising discipline that was meant to correct them and to call them back to repentance and obedience so that they would "not be condemned with the world" (v. 32).[2]

In other words, God brought a *temporal* judgment upon them. I use the word *temporal* on purpose, since *final* judgment for a Christian was already paid for at the cross. But this kind of judgment is still serious because their sin apparently rendered them useless for further service to Christ, and he decided their lives were over.

Further, because the communion service is such a special practice of the church, the Lord may also have wanted to send a message that sin is a serious offense to the holiness of God, especially when we are participating in a ceremony that is meant to remember the sacrifice Christ made to deliver us from that sin.

The church has an obligation to pursue purity and embrace a life of repentance. But if someone refuses to repent of sin, then that unrepentant person is demonstrating a lack of true saving faith, which would ultimately result in condemnation. In this sense, one who would refuse to repent would be considered apostate, and would demonstrate that they were never truly saved to begin with (see 1 John 2:19).

Because the church was not exercising church discipline (see Matthew 18:15–20; 1 Corinthians 5) and confronting this serious sin, God decided to step in and take matters into his own hands. This is very frightening, and should serve as a warning to the church so that we do not take a casual and flippant attitude toward sin.

Unfortunately, some Christians may go down paths of sin that could do irreparable harm to themselves, the witness of the church, and the reputation of Christ. This story may seem to suggest that before any more harm is done, God may choose to intervene in discipline.

Now, this doesn't mean that in every situation where there is illness and death in a Christian's life, it is always connected to some form of divine discipline for sin (even though that's what happened here). That surely wasn't the case for Paul's "thorn" that caused him to become weak (2 Corinthians 12). The purpose of the "thorn" (whatever it may have been) was to keep Paul humble, not to chastise him for sin, and he was told that he should rely on God's sufficient grace to sustain him.

But in Corinth, the illness and weakness were directly related to sin. So there are several reasons why this story is in the Bible. It serves as a warning to the church about having a flippant attitude toward sin, especially a sin that is destructive to the church's witness to the world. It further highlights the seriousness of God's call to the unity and purity of the church, witnessed to by their ongoing participation in the Lord's Supper, which is designed to remind them of Christ's sacrifice in delivering them from sin.

And finally, it reminds us that there may be some in the church who are not true believers after all, and that we can recognize them by their unrepentance and warn them about the condemnation that awaits those who refuse to repent and receive the grace and forgiveness so freely offered to and experienced by whosoever believes.

22

A Youth Group
Is Killed by Bears

There are some stories you read in the Bible that are incredulous and shocking—at least on the surface. Further digging will always assist in getting perspective, but some stories still leave you speechless. A perfect example comes from the Old Testament book of 2 Kings, where the newly appointed prophet Elisha is beginning his ministry.

> From there Elisha went up to Bethel. As he was walking up the path, some small boys came out of the city and jeered at him, chanting, "Go up, baldy! Go up, baldy!" He turned around, looked at them, and cursed them in the name of the LORD. Then two female bears came out of the woods and mauled forty-two of the children. From there Elisha went to Mount Carmel, and then he returned to Samaria.
>
> *2 Kings 2:23–24*

What in the world?! I remember what it was like to be a kid. Kids often teased each other with little singsong mockeries, like when we picked up a dandelion and said, "Missy had a baby and its head popped off," while flicking the dandelion from its stem. Though it was rather juvenile, insensitive, and perhaps a little cruel, it was not something that made one *worthy of death*.

So when we read the above Scripture that some boys were jeering at a prophet, making fun of his hairlessness, and he reciprocates with a curse and two angry bears, we are left with our mouths open. I realize some people are sensitive about hair loss, but was Elisha having a bad day or what? Once again, a fuller context will help us shed light on this story.

These are dark times for the nation of Israel. We have a divided kingdom, rampant idolatry amongst God's people, and corrupt leadership breathing threats toward the LORD's prophets. The wicked king and queen of Israel, Ahab and Jezebel, have both recently died, and Ahab's sons will take over. First it was Ahaziah, who was worse than his father, who reigned briefly but died due to injuries from a fall.[1] Later, his brother, Jehoram, takes over in the Northern Kingdom of Israel. He's no good either.

Meanwhile, Israel is almost constantly at war with its main rival in Syria, aka the Arameans, and they are still all about worshiping and consulting the pagan god Baal. Elijah had put to death 450 prophets of Baal on Mount Carmel after a dramatic display of God's power (see 1 Kings 18). But Elijah's ministry had come to an end; it was time to pass the torch, so to speak, to his protégé Elisha.

In a miraculous event, Elijah is escorted by angels to heaven, and a double portion of his prophetic power is left on Elisha, who then begins his ministry as the lead prophet of Israel. After an initial test of his power with the cloak of Elijah (which he used to part the waters of the Jordan River), Elisha is affirmed by another band of godly prophets called the "sons of the prophets," which is a group of prophets who would often meet for study, worship, and mutual encouragement. They recognize him as Elijah's formal replacement.

Elisha then performs another miracle in response to a request from the men of the city of Jericho, and heals the waters of the city that had previously been under a curse from the time of Joshua's conquest. Interestingly, Elisha's first two miracles involve the waters of the Jordan and the springs of Jericho, whereby water is a source of life. Could this be the dawn of a new age of spiritual life for God's people with Elisha leading the way?

It is here that we meet up with our story about Elisha's power and authority being challenged by those hostile to God's people. Elisha is on his way to Bethel, an Israelite city that had abandoned the LORD and had become thoroughly corrupt, engaging in all kinds of pagan worship. In fact, it was one of the places where one of Israel's previous kings—Jeroboam—had set up a golden calf for Israel to worship.

> From there [Jericho] Elisha went up to Bethel. As he was walking up the path, some small boys came out of the city and jeered at him, chanting, "Go up, baldy! Go up, baldy!"
>
> 2 Kings 2:23

You might see the words *small boys*, and think of eight- or nine-year-old kids who are just acting silly. But that is not the case. Though the translation from Hebrew to English says "small boys," perhaps the words "young lads" would actually be better. In fact, the Hebrew word can refer to any males ages twelve to thirty, so this changes the way we should look at it. These were a band of bad boys from Bethel, perhaps even a gang of bandits in their late teens or early twenties, who had no respect for the prophet.

In fact, their mocking and jeering should be perceived as an imminent threat to the prophet's safety.[2] And it is what they said to him that made it clear that they did not want him there. Their cry of "go up, baldy!" must be further explained. It is possible that Elisha had shaved his head denoting his role as a prophet, or it could have been some physical marking that was unique to him (like a bald spot). Either way, the young lads were using the word to scorn him.

Further, their shout of "go up" must be heard with contempt; it is not referring to the idea that he should "go up" to Bethel. Rather, they want him to "go up" to heaven just like his predecessor Elijah did. They want him gone, to disappear. They wanted nothing to do with this prophet of Israel or the God he represented.

We then see what Elisha does next.

> He turned around, looked at them, and cursed them in the name of the LORD.
>
> 2 Kings 2:24

Elijah pronounced a curse on them. This idea of a curse is not something foreign to Israel's experiences. Back in Deuteronomy 28, when Moses was leading the Israelites, a covenant was made between them and God at Mount Sinai. Part of that covenant involved both blessings for obedience (Deuteronomy 28:1–14) and curses in the case of disobedience (Deuteronomy 28:15–68) to God's prescribed laws and commands.

At this point, Israel had turned its back on the LORD and pursued the gods of the foreign nations, notably Baal. So Israel was to experience many of the curses outlined in the Mosaic covenant due to her disobedience. So when Elisha encounters the hostile group, it is no surprise to see that the prophet put a curse specifically on these young men as a pronouncement of judgment. And judgment came . . .

> Then two female bears came out of the woods and mauled forty-two of the children [or "young lads"].

Elisha's curse on them was his call for God to deal with them as the LORD saw fit, and the punishment of the LORD was death, since ridiculing Elisha was the same as ridiculing the LORD. Ultimately, it was the LORD who was responsible for the creative type of judgment that fell on them. This would have served as a warning to all who might try to interfere with or undercut this prophet's ministry. Biblical scholar Paul R. House states, "The youths were typical of a nation that 'mocked God's messengers, despised his words and scoffed at his prophets' (2 Chronicles 36:16)."[3]

So the curse was not merely a warning to the local population; it was a warning to the nation as a whole. God will not tolerate the unfaithfulness of his people who make themselves liable to judgment due to their apostasy. Israel should take heed. There is a prophet of God in the land, and he means business.

This is yet another example of how the Bible teaches us that God is holy, sovereign, all-powerful, and has the right to execute justice and judgment at his discretion, and Israel was worthy of it. Thankfully, those who by faith are God's people today never have to fear God's ultimate judgment, for the penalty for our sins was already exacted on and paid for by our Savior when he was punished on the cross for our sins.

Putting this story in that wider context softens our objections somewhat. God is not arbitrarily causing children to be mauled to death simply for teasing a bald man out for a walk. Rather, a corrupt, hostile, and threatening group of young men wished that the LORD's chosen prophet were dead or gone so that they could continue their sensual idolatry without interruption. Never mind what Moses said centuries earlier. Never mind the covenant Israel swore to abide by. These Israelites wanted their sin and, as a result, they reaped the harvest associated with it.

23

Not Peace but Division

In the Old Testament, Isaiah prophesied that the Messiah to come would be known as the "Prince of Peace" (Isaiah 9:6). He would bring peace and embody peace. The concept of peace (Hebrew—*shalom*; Greek—*eirēnē*) is deeply rooted in the Hebrew-Christian Scriptures and psyche, and is a predominate principle (1 Samuel 25:6) and pertinent prayer (Numbers 6:26) throughout the pages of both the Old and New Testaments. The apostles Peter and Paul both use and speak of it in all their letters to the churches. It communicates the idea of wholeness, completeness, security, well-being (prosperity), and the end of hostility.

Jesus' statement in both Matthew 10:34 and Luke 12:51 that he did not come to "bring peace" on the earth seems to contradict Isaiah's prophecy and even the announcement of the angels to the shepherds in Luke 2:14. What's more, Jesus likely repeated this idea on more than one occasion, as Matthew records him as saying he did not come to bring peace "but a sword," and Luke records him as saying that instead of peace there would be "division."

This doesn't seem to make sense on the surface, especially if Jesus is indeed the "Prince of Peace" who brought us the "gospel of Peace" (Ephesians 6:15) so that we may have "peace with God" (Romans 5:1) and "peace in our hearts and minds" (Philippians 4:7) while we strive for "peace with one another" (Romans 12:18).

Did not Jesus promise his disciples at the Last Supper that he would leave them with and give them his "peace" (John 14:26), an otherworldly type of peace that would comfort and strengthen the otherwise unconfident and fearful heart? Indeed he did.

Why would Jesus seem to speak otherwise in these two other occasions in Matthew and Luke? The key to understanding and reconciling these passages with the rest of the Bible is to see them both in their context. In both Matthew 10 and Luke 12, Jesus is communicating the cost of following him. It will come with a price tag attached and it will cost them more than they can imagine, even *at times* the things that they hold near and dear. For Jesus says in Matthew 10,

> "Do not think that I have come to bring peace to the earth. I have not come to bring peace, but a sword. For I have come to set a man against his father, and a daughter against her mother, and a daughter-in-law against her mother-in-law. And a person's enemies will be those of his own household."
>
> Matthew 10:34–36 ESV

Similarly, in Luke 12 Jesus states,

> "Do you think that I have come to give peace on earth? No, I tell you, but rather division. For from now on in one house there will be five divided, three against two and two against three. They will be divided, father against son and son against father, mother against daughter and daughter against mother, mother-in-law against her daughter-in-law and daughter-in-law against mother-in-law."
>
> Luke 12:51–53 ESV

What's shocking in both of these texts is that being a disciple of Christ will undoubtedly have the effect of dividing up families, pitting unbelievers against believers, such that unity on matters of a spiritual nature will become an impossibility. A follower of Christ will espouse differing convictions on matters of life and faith that will naturally exclude them from agreement with members of their own family.

This does not mean it is impossible to have healthy relationships, but it does mean that conflict concerning the deepest matters of the Christian faith will naturally occur between those who are following Christ faithfully and those who are not. In fact, one should be prepared for hostility on many levels, especially concerning matters of life and practice. Jesus did not want his disciples to be unprepared for the implications of believing in and following him faithfully.

In his classic book entitled *The Hard Sayings of Jesus*, the late New Testament scholar F. F. Bruce summarizes the sense of these passages perfectly and speaks of the implications of Christ's words:

> So, when Jesus said that he had come to bring "not peace but a sword," he meant that this would be the *effect* of his coming, not that it was the *purpose* of his coming. His words came true in the life of the early Church, and they have verified themselves subsequently in the history of Christian missions. Where one or two members of a family or other social group have accepted the Christian faith, this has repeatedly provoked opposition from other members.[1]

These sayings by Christ should cause every Christian to look at their lives introspectively to see if they are living the faithful Christian life that naturally brings opposition from a world filled with darkness.

The apostle John told us, "Do not be surprised, brothers and sisters, if the world hates you" (1 John 3:13). And Jesus told us elsewhere:

"If the world hates you, know that it has hated me before it hated you. If you were of the world, the world would love you as its own; but because you are not of the world, but I chose you out of the world, therefore the world hates you. Remember the word that I said to you: 'A servant is not greater than his master.' If they persecuted me, they will also persecute you. . . ."

John 15:18–20 ESV

Faithful Christianity is bound to live counterculturally to the fallen world where the value systems, convictions, and activities are diametrically opposed to a biblical worldview. Christ-followers should feel like "aliens and strangers" (1 Peter 2:11) in a world that is not their true home or final destination. We are technically "citizens of heaven" (Philippians 3:20) who are just passing through.

Let us consider the cost of following Jesus. Are you willing to be mocked, cast out, ridiculed, marginalized, or in some instances killed? He who loses his life for Christ's sake will surely find it.

So is there peace? Yes. Peace with God and peace within the family of God. But if you are truly following in the footsteps of Jesus and loving him more than the world, expect some division, and in some instances even a sword.

24

Absalom's Head
Stuck in a Tree

The Bible reflects life as we know it, both good and bad. There is little that we experience today that isn't already found in the pages of Scripture. People are people due to our sin nature being passed on through the generations.

One of the more devastating sins is that of betrayal. Yes, sins such as sexual sin and murder are treacherous and can wreak havoc on relationships. But betrayal is its own kind of heinousness. It is a violation of a sacred trust that at one time existed between two people who lived in relationship with one another.

The most prominent example of betrayal in Scripture is that of Judas Iscariot, one of the original twelve disciples, who betrayed Jesus for thirty pieces of silver. He is even known as the "betrayer" (Matthew 26:46, 48; 27:3; Mark 14:42, 44). It is hard to imagine that a man who once walked with Jesus, who saw all of his miracles, listened to his teaching, and experienced great blessing would turn away in unbelief, be possessed by Satan, and even take his own life. But this is the nature of sin. It destroys everything it touches, especially relationships.

Another painful instance of betrayal is found in the Old Testament. Rather than a betrayal of friendship, it is a betrayal of family. It is the story of David and Absalom.

King David was known as a man after God's own heart (1 Samuel 13:14; Acts 13:22). In spite of this affirmation, David was a sinner like you and me. His list of sins is on full display, and include adultery, murder, deceit, polygamy, passivity to the rape of his own daughter by another son, and pride.

Yet David's deep regret over his sins is also seen plainly in Scripture. Psalm 51 contains his confession to God following the sins he committed with Bathsheba.[1] God's grace followed David and cleansed him from sin. Still, the consequences of his sinful choices were devastating. The prophet Nathan told David that "the sword will never depart from your house" (2 Samuel 12:10), and many subsequent narratives demonstrate that humiliation, death, divisiveness, and betrayal did follow David and his descendants. David's son from Bathsheba died in infancy. But one of the most grievous consequences of David's sins came at the hands of his third son, Absalom, whose betrayal of his father is legendary.

We are told that King David had at least eight wives (at least these are the ones that are named). It is possible he had even more (see 2 Samuel 5:13). This is itself a sin against God, because God ordained from the beginning that marriage is to be between *one* man and *one* woman in a covenant relationship that is designed to last a lifetime. Therefore, polygamy is a violation of the moral will of God.

Many of David's marriages were for the purposes of forming political alliances and treaties with surrounding nations (in direct violation of Deuteronomy 17:17), and this was likely the case with David's wife Maacah (2 Samuel 3:3).

Maacah bore him a son named Absalom, who was said to be incredibly handsome. He would get a haircut once a year, and

Scripture says "from the sole of his foot to the crown of his head there was no blemish on him" (2 Samuel 14:25 ESV). As you can imagine, he was quite popular among the people.

Absalom also had a beautiful sister, Tamar, who became the incestuous lust of David's firstborn son named Amnon, a son born from another of David's wives. As her half brother, Amnon eventually rapes Tamar in order to fulfill his lust. But when David hears about it, he only expresses anger and chooses not to punish Amnon. His ambivalence to the rape of his daughter is yet another one of David's shortcomings and sins.

Meanwhile, Absalom, David's son and Tamar's full brother, takes his sister in to stay with him and begins to plot the death of Amnon for violating Tamar. Two years later, Absalom finally gets his revenge and has Amnon assassinated. Absalom then flees to the land of his grandfather, and remains there for three years to let the situation die down.

Eventually, David begins to miss Absalom, even though he was responsible for killing Amnon. Time has a way of healing wounds, and perhaps David even understood why Absalom did what he did (to a point). This doesn't excuse Absalom for what he did, since two wrongs don't make a right, but at least David was still interested in having a relationship with his popular yet murderous son.

In time, and through some maneuvering, Absalom is allowed back to Jerusalem but is not allowed to come into the king's presence, per David's instructions. Perhaps some time to think and repent would be good for Absalom. But the time away did nothing but frustrate Absalom, as he felt cut off from the privileges of being the king's son.

He finds a way to manipulate Joab (the king's nephew who also became the commander of the army) into giving him an opportunity to appear before the king, and Absalom and David are reunited, though Absalom still refuses to repent. Below the surface he is still angry at his father for doing nothing after his sister was raped. His resentment will be the seed to a rebellion and a revolt, and he begins to use his handsome appearance, charisma, and popularity to draw people toward him while undermining his father, King David, and publicly shaming him for his lack of justice.

Samuel tells us that Absalom "stole the hearts of the men of Israel" (2 Samuel 15:6 ESV). David was aging, occupied with other matters, and was not engaged with the people like Absalom was. After four years of drumming up support and fame, the plan for a coup was set into motion. Absalom even successfully recruited David's personal counselor to side with him.

After David discovers the plot, he prepares to flee Jerusalem, the city he loves. He doesn't want Absalom to destroy him or his house, so he takes off, leaving behind ten concubines to manage the homestead. In this moment, David is rightly afraid and pens these words: "Rise up, LORD! Save me, my God! You strike all my enemies on the cheek; you break the teeth of the wicked" (Psalm 3:7).

So David leaves Jerusalem, weeping, knowing in his heart that much of this is due to the consequences of his past sins. Meanwhile, Absalom arrives at David's house, which was empty except for the ten concubines left behind. As a sign of asserting his power and to humiliate his father, Absalom has sexual relations with David's harem on the palace roof, thus sealing his claim to the throne for all to see.

Meanwhile, David and his entourage escape and cross the Jordan River to the east and are cared for by the people living there. But Absalom and the commander of his army also cross the Jordan. As they pursue David, he musters up a formidable army from the valiant men who are with him, and he tells his commanders to go out and meet them in battle but to deal gently with Absalom since he is the king's son.

The two armies—divided countrymen—battle in a forest. David's army prevails, killing some twenty thousand men from Absalom's army. As Absalom flees, one is hardly prepared to read what happens next.

> Absalom was riding on his mule when he happened to meet David's soldiers. When the mule went under the tangled branches of a large

oak tree, Absalom's head was caught fast in the tree. The mule under him kept going, so he was suspended in midair.

2 Samuel 18:9

How ironic. The popular, handsome, treasonous son who thought so highly of himself gets his head caught in a tree, dangling and vulnerable. Sin has a way of making a fool of us (see Joshua 7:26 concerning Achan's sin), and this time it had its way with Absalom. The hair on Absalom, which Samuel tells us about (14:26), may have been his undoing, or perhaps Absalom had a large head, causing it to lodge in the branches.

Either way, upon hearing about this, Joab, one of David's commanders, finds Absalom suspended from the tree and thrusts three javelins into his chest. Joab's armor-bearers finish Absalom off with a sword, throw his body into a pit, and pile a mountain of stones on it—a fitting end to someone who attempted to steal something that wasn't theirs.

Though David requested it, there was no mercy for Absalom. And despite his son's rebellion and betrayal, David cries out, "O my son Absalom, my son, my son Absalom! Would I have died instead of you, O Absalom, my son, my son!" (2 Samuel 18:33 ESV). It didn't have to be this way.

So why is this story in the Bible? There may be multiple reasons, but we can hardly miss the obvious: Sin destroys. It destroys homes, relationships, legacies, and almost everything it touches. But God still had a plan, and in spite of David's sin, God gracefully delivered him from it.

For the sake of the Lord's name, he preserved David's life. It will be through David's other son, Solomon (and not Absalom), that the line to the Messiah would be established. And the amount of patience and grace that God extended to David is remarkable, though sin surely had its consequences.

These stories and many others like it in the Bible serve as a warning to us, written for our instruction, so that we may not desire the evil things that people did in Bible times (Hebrews 10: 6, 11). May stories like this keep us humble, deter us from sin, and cause us to rejoice in the never-ending grace of God so that we can keep from getting a "big head." Sin has a way of hanging us out to dry, making us weak and vulnerable, and leading us down the path toward death. Just ask Absalom.

In the words of the writer of Hebrews, we must stand up to sin's enticements, and

> Let him who thinks he stands take heed lest he fall.
>
> Hebrews 10:12 NKJV

25

The Sun and Moon Stand Still

≡ JOSHUA 10:12–14 ≡

As a book that records the revelation of God to humanity, the Bible is filled with stories that tell of miraculous events of a supernatural God who has broken into our world. Stories such as the creation of the world, the parting of the Red Sea, and the resurrection of Jesus Christ are but a few of the miraculous moments.

Those who tend to dismiss any form of supernaturalism see the Scriptures as mere fantasy, made-up fables that have no correlation to scientific reality. But even science itself lacks adequate explanations for things it cannot sort out, and it often changes its mind. A theory will often become "fact" if it is politically expedient to be so, until some new information comes along that replaces those "facts" with an even newer theory.

But when all the facts are fully known in the truest sense, the Bible will stand the test of time as a historically accurate portrayal of reality and miracles. Yes, I believe that miracles still happen today (primarily in response to prayer) that even doctors cannot explain. The cancer was just there yesterday, but today no one can explain where it went.

In the minds of unbelievers, Christians believe some of the strangest things—that God created the world out of nothing, that one day Jesus Christ will return in the clouds riding on a white horse, that the world as we know it will be destroyed one day by fire and a new heaven and new earth will be formed where immortal believers will live for all eternity in resurrected, glorified bodies.

But these stories of supernatural and miraculous nature are the foundational events in the story line of our redemption from sin by a supernatural God. And one of the more interesting story lines in the history of redemption of God's people comes from the Old Testament book of Joshua, where Joshua, the leader of the Israelites, is leading God's people into the Promised Land as they defeat and conquer the Canaanites, who refused to repent, thus becoming worthy of God's judgment.

Hundreds of years earlier, God had promised this land to Abraham and his descendants. Generations later, following the death of Moses, who led God's people out of bondage in Egypt, Moses' successor, Joshua, leads the next generation of faithful Israelites to take possession of the land.

Crossing the Jordan River from the east, Joshua marches forward with the ark of the covenant (a symbol of God's presence) in the lead. As soon as the feet of the priests touch the water, the waters of the full flowing river stop ("rose up in a heap very far away"—Joshua 3:16 ESV) and the priests and the people are able to cross the riverbed on dry ground. This miracle, similar to the crossing of the Red Sea under Moses, paves the way for future miracles that God will do in the foreseeable conquest of the land, most notably the conquering of the walled city of Jericho in Joshua 6.

Recorded in Joshua 10, one of the most astounding victories experienced by Israel is "the day the sun and the moon stood still." The Israelites were well under way in their conquest of the land. Their strategy had been to divide and conquer. After a minor setback due to disobedience, the Israelites eventually wiped out the city of Ai and its inhabitants. This caused many of the other Canaanite nations and their kings to panic, and they began to unite to fight Joshua and the Israelites.

Meanwhile, one of the nations, the Hivites, got creative. Coming from one of their cities known as Gibeon, they pretended to be someone they were not. They decided to put together a unique caravan that would go out to meet Joshua. They tore their clothes in order to appear worn-out, put patched sandals on their feet, grabbed old sackcloths for their donkeys, and put together wineskins that looked torn and mended. They brought crusty bread and pretended they were from a faraway country that had heard of the amazing God of Israel and how he had delivered them from all their enemies. They offered themselves as servants to Israel and requested to make a covenant of peace with Israel.

The trick worked, as Joshua seemingly had compassion on them and made a covenant treaty not to destroy them. He failed to ask God about them first and, as a result, they were spared. However, once the truth was found out, they were cursed by Joshua and consigned to be woodcutters and carriers of water on account of their deception.

The other Canaanite tribes were furious with the people of Gibeon, and a coalition of five Amorite kings went out to attack them because they had "wimped out" and failed to stand up to Israel. The Gibeonites cried out to Israel for help, and because of Israel's foolish covenant with them, they were on the hook to protect them. But Israel was no worse for wear, because God was with them in great power.

While Israel was engaged in a successful battle, the Bible says that God threw large hailstones from the sky onto the enemy as they were fleeing down the side of a mountain.

> As they fled before Israel, the LORD threw large hailstones on them from the sky along the descent of Beth-horon all the way to Azekah, and they died. More of them died from the hail than the Israelites killed with the sword.
>
> Joshua 10:11

God was going to battle with Israel, but the miracle of the day was yet to come. Joshua sought the LORD in prayer in order to finish the job. What he asked for was seemingly impossible—yet he was praying to the God of the supernatural who can routinely do the impossible.

On the day the LORD gave the Amorites over to the Israelites, Joshua spoke to the LORD in the presence of Israel:

"Sun, stand still over Gibeon, and moon, over the Valley of Aijalon." And the sun stood still and the moon stopped until the nation took vengeance on its enemies. Isn't this written in the Book of Jashar? So the sun stopped in the middle of the sky and delayed its setting almost a full day.

There has been no day like it before or since, when the LORD listened to a man, because the LORD fought for Israel. Then Joshua and all Israel with him returned to the camp at Gilgal.

Joshua 10:12–14[1]

It was high noon ("The sun stopped in the middle of the sky") when Joshua prayed. He knew he needed more time, and God gave it. In what is a scientific miracle, somehow the LORD caused the rotation of the earth to cease such that the sun and moon (likely off in the horizon) stayed in their place so that Joshua and his army could finish the battle.

Speculation runs rampant on what might have happened. Some suggest it is merely poetic and not a literal halt of the sun and moon, but this would put all other battle narratives in question in such a way that would cause us to doubt whether any of the Bible was true instead of some kind of creative fiction. How would one sort out that which is literal from that which is figurative?

Some have suggested it was an eclipse of some type or a refraction of light to make it seem like the day was going on longer after the eclipse subsided. But that's not convincing either, since the text says that the sun delayed setting for almost an entire day. Other ideas have been set forth, but none compare to simply taking the text at face value.

God, the maker of heaven and earth, has authority over nature, just like Jesus did when he calmed the wind and the waves and raised people from the dead. He can suspend the laws of nature and science, and he can rain down hailstones on the specific side of a hill and cause the sun and the moon to stand still.

Would other catastrophic events have happened if the earth's rotation stopped? Surely, yes. Tidal waves, earthquakes, and so on. God would have had to handle all of that too. But there again, he is a God of miracles.

With a little further digging, another reason surfaces as to why God may have done this miracle. Writing in the notable *Bible Knowledge Commentary*, biblical scholars John Walvoord and Roy Zuck tell us:

> An important fact that should not be overlooked is that the sun and the moon were the principal deities among the Canaanites. At the prayer of Israel's leader Canaan's gods were compelled to obey. This disturbance to their gods must have been terribly upsetting and frightening to the Canaanites.[2]

This is clearly one reason why this is in the Bible—not only to recount the historical fact of a dramatic miracle in answer to prayer, but also to demonstrate the supremacy of Israel's one true God in comparison to the false gods of paganism. The LORD once again showed to all Israel and to her enemies that there is no one like him.

Joshua and his men ended up winning the day—a very long day—and put to death all their enemies. The five kings of the Amorites fled into a cave but were subdued and brought out before Israel. Joshua had his commanders put their feet on the kings' necks (a sign of complete conquest and humiliation of one's enemy), and Joshua struck them down and left them hanging until evening (eventually the sun did set).

The victory was finally theirs, and God fought for them and intervened with incredulous authority over nature. Hundreds of years later, God would go to war again, sending his own Son to conquer sin on our behalf, and once again he would suspend the laws of nature in multiple ways, the most important of which was his resurrection from the dead. He will stop short of nothing to redeem his people. And for those who seek him, they will always come out winners.

26

"Neither Jew nor Gentile . . . Male nor Female"

GALATIANS 3:27–28

We live in a confused world. This, of course, is what Satan wants. There is a reason why he is called a liar (John 8:44) and a deceiver (Revelation 12:9). He aims to cause complete chaos within the realm that God has created, especially among human beings. Satan is very successful at causing destruction, corruption, and confusion at all levels of society, from institutions to societal structures to families and individual relationships.

But even though Satan is called the "prince *of this world*" (John 12:31)—meaning prince of the evil world system we live in today—he is not the all-powerful, mighty, and sovereign God of the universe who is ultimately in control and has a plan to redeem humankind from sin and death's hold. In fact, Jesus' death and resurrection assure us that Satan is a defeated foe even though for now he is very active in the world in which we live.

One place Satan is wreaking havoc is in the area of one's personal identity. His successful assaults on sexual identity, sexual orientation, godly sexuality, and gender roles have had a dramatic impact on Western society. His aim is to strip us of a proper understanding of what it means to be made in the image of God, to be made male and female, and to understand the privileges and respective roles that go along with those identities.

Though many might say that the Industrial Revolution of the eighteenth and nineteenth centuries was the greatest revolution in Western history, one could argue that the sexual revolution that we are currently in today has far eclipsed it in terms of significance and scope. Today, "anyone who holds to a traditional biblical understanding of human sexuality . . . is now simply out of bounds in contemporary society."[1]

Contemporary secular thought on sexuality, gender, and role distinctions is driven more by the futile thinking of a depraved mind (Romans 1:21, 28) and the sensual affections of the flesh (Romans 1:21, 24, 26) instead of biblical revelation, natural law, or science. Though some doctors and scientists are attempting to argue that there is a difference between sex and gender (sex being referred to as anatomy and gender as one's subjective sense of identity based on psychological dispositions), the Bible is clear that there are only two genders—male and female (Genesis 1:27)—and that our sense of identity and the roles we play are uniquely aligned with our biology (Genesis 2:18, 21–24; 1 Corinthians 11:7–9; Ephesians 5:22–33; 1 Timothy 2:12–14).

This means then that the confusion we face in the world when it comes to matters of sexual identity and behavior, or even psychological disorders such as gender dysphoria, are all symptoms of living in a fallen and depraved world where our desires and perceptions have all been tainted by sin. In fact, the Bible teaches that we are *totally depraved*, meaning that "the corruption of original sin extends to every aspect of human nature: to one's reason and will as well as to one's appetites and impulses."[2]

Therefore, the mass confusion our world experiences is perfectly explainable, and the Bible must serve as our guide and corrective so that we can rightly understand what it means to be made in the image of God and made to be male and female. But what do we do with verses like Galatians 3:27–28 that seemingly wash out identities or role distinctions between men and women? Indeed, some have used these verses to completely cleanse Christianity from male-female distinctions and roles, both in a general sense as well as in a specific sense relative to roles played in the family and in the church.

But before we put these verses in their proper context, let's see them for ourselves so we know what we are dealing with. Paul wrote to the Galatian church,

> For those of you who were baptized into Christ have been clothed with Christ. There is no Jew or Greek, slave or free, male and female; since you are all one in Christ Jesus.
>
> Galatians 3:27–28

It is important to first note what the Scripture actually says while we also put it into its proper context. When Paul speaks of baptism here, he is not talking about water baptism per se, but rather about our spiritual cleansing that comes by faith that places us in a spiritual union with Christ (or a "spiritual immersion into Christ"). This spiritual cleansing and immersion "into" Christ happens at the moment we repent of sin and place our faith and trust in him alone for our salvation.

This profound spiritual union with Jesus means that his perfect life, sacrificial death, and miraculous resurrection are all credited to our spiritual account in such a way that we are positionally seen as perfect before God. In this sense we have been "clothed with Christ." His life becomes our life, his death becomes our death, and his resurrection becomes our resurrection. All that he has, we have. All that he accomplished is credited to us. It is truly an amazing truth.

We still have to grow spiritually on the path of becoming more like him, and we will never be perfect in a practical sense in this life. But spiritually speaking, we have all the spiritual riches that can be found in the person of Christ. And as Paul said in Romans 10,

> Everyone who believes on him will not be put to shame, since there is no distinction between Jew and Greek, because the same Lord of all richly blesses all who call on him. For everyone who calls on the name of the Lord will be saved.
>
> Romans 10:11–13

Notice who Paul says will receive the rich spiritual blessings that can be found in Christ? *Everyone who calls on the name of the Lord*, both Jew and Greek (or Gentile). In other words, in Christ there is no distinction between a Jew or a Gentile. Both stand equally before God as redeemed children of God without favor or distinction when it comes to salvation.

This is exactly what Paul is saying earlier in our Galatians passage as well, except he expands it to all the other categories that are often divided up and at times can even be separated in the world's eyes. Whether it is a slave or a free person, whether it is a male or a female, all have equal access and all can share in the privileges of salvation that come to us by faith in Christ.

Elsewhere in Colossians, he told them something similar and expanded it differently to include even more people groups that one would never guess would be equally a part of the family of God.

> You are being renewed in knowledge according to the image of your Creator. In Christ there is not Greek and Jew, circumcision and uncircumcision, barbarian, Scythian, slave and free; but Christ is all and in all.
>
> Colossians 3:10–11

Christ is everything. It's all about him, and when you are "included" in Christ through a spiritual union that comes by faith, you are a child of God who is being renewed in the image of God. Period. In all these passages we quoted, take special notice of the idea that you are "not this" or "not that." When it comes to *salvation*, there is no status or distinction or ethnicity that makes you different from anyone else. All are equal in essence before Christ.

But we must understand, the context of these verses is talking about our oneness in and with Christ that is uniquely tied to our *salvation*. Salvation is the subject, and mistakes are made in biblical interpretation when we step outside the context and try to apply it to modern-day agendas that the text is not even speaking about or to.

This passage *does not say* there is no such thing as an ethnic distinction in the church. It *does not say* there is no such thing as a male or a female anymore, or that there is no longer any respective roles that men and women uniquely play in the home or in the church. To be sure, the Bible celebrates ethnicity as it brings glory to the Christ who was slain. In Revelation 5, they are singing a new song:

> And they sang a new song: You are worthy to take the scroll and to open its seals, because you were slaughtered, and you purchased people for God by your blood from every tribe and language and people and nation. You made them a kingdom and priests to our God, and they will reign on the earth.
>
> Revelation 5:9–10

Further, the Bible also keeps male and female distinctions and roles, as Paul said that husbands are to "love your wives just as Christ loved the church" (Ephesians 5:25) and that the "husband is the head of the wife" (Ephesians 5:23—referring to spiritual leadership). In the same way, wives are to "submit to your husbands as to the Lord" (Ephesians 5:22). Though it is beyond the scope of this chapter, we could go even further and talk about the unique roles that men and women were designed to play in the church (see 1 Timothy 2:12–15; 3:1–13; Titus 2:2–6). Simply put, men and women are different, and being a Christian who is "in Christ" does not change that. As Christian ethicist Andrew Walker has rightly said,

> Men and women are different at the deepest levels of their being. Our chromosomes are different. Our brains are different. Our voices are different. Our body shapes are different. Our body strengths are different. Our reproductive systems are different. The design for what our bodies are structured and destined for are different, and these designs bear witness to differences that reflect God's creative will for humanity.[3]

Because this is true, we should never lose those specific and unique distinctions that make us uniquely what God made us to be, and though Satan may try to rob us of this through the cultural winds that are blowing, we must stand firm on the truth of God's Word. For the world's wisdom is foolishness compared to the wisdom of God (1 Corinthians 1:18–24).

Let's be clear. Galatians 3:27–28, Romans 10:11–13, or Colossians 3:10–11 cannot be used as "proof texts" to flatten out ethnic identities, biological identities, or role distinctions in the family or the church. These verses refer to the subject of *our salvation in Christ*. We are all equally children of God, brothers and sisters in Christ, and our true identity is found in Jesus.[4] It is an *exclusive* gospel message (John 14:6) with an incredibly *inclusive* scope, such that "whosoever believes" in him (John 3:16) will not perish but will have everlasting life.

27

Ananias and Sapphira

When the Holy Spirit was poured out in fullness on the church in the book of Acts, an amazing sense of unity and blessing fell on the early followers of Christ. For the first time, the Spirit of God resided fully *within* the believing people of God as a whole, enabling them to experience abundant grace.

While the apostles were performing many miracles (Acts 2:43), a sense of awe and wonder filled the church, along with sweet, joyful fellowship (2:46). Further, a devotion to "earth-shaking prayer" helped bring about a "boldness in witnessing" for Christ (4:31). Nothing like this had ever been experienced before. The believers shared in regular daily worship and were committed to sharing their lives, their homes, and their possessions with anyone who had need. The spiritual blessings it brought were unparalleled.

In Acts 4 we see the church praying and preaching and fully unified with "one heart and soul" (verse 32 ESV). A sense of self-lessness pervaded the church, and as needs among them surfaced,

people were willing to go as far as selling their own land in order
to help. Luke tells us,

> For there was not a needy person among them because all those
> who owned lands or houses sold them, brought the proceeds of
> what was sold, and laid them at the apostles' feet. This was then
> distributed to each person as any had need.
>
> Acts 4:34–35

No doubt some of these new believers lost their jobs or busi-
nesses due to their willingness to follow Christ, as public persecution and even exile from many unbelieving families must have
existed. But the church came to their aid, and this kind of self-
sacrificial generosity was based on the philosophy that whatever
someone owned ultimately belonged to God. If God wanted to
use their material possessions to help someone who was destitute,
it should be used for that purpose.

This wasn't mandated but rather was voluntary. And the generosity was astounding, even liquidating real estate and assets, some
of which may have been a part of the family inheritance for years.

This is what genuine love looks like. The apostle John would
later comment,

> If anyone has this world's goods and sees a fellow believer in need
> but withholds compassion from him—how does God's love reside
> in him?
>
> 1 John 3:17

What the church was experiencing in Acts 4 was nothing less
than the love of God being shared among brethren. No wonder
the fellowship was sweet. People were giving, which always brings
joy, and people were receiving, yet another aspect of God's grace.

Luke points out that even Barnabas, who would later become
Paul's ministry companion on his first missionary journey, was
willing to sell a tract of land in order to contribute. Since Barnabas's name means "encouragement," it is clear that his actions

helped him live up to his name, as his sacrifice would have encouraged many in need.

This was a crucial time in the fledgling church's history, a time where the foundation of the church was being built through the spread of the gospel and the teaching of the apostles—teaching and doctrine that would eventually become our New Testament Scriptures.

It is not surprising that a spiritual attack from the evil one would be imminent. It would be like Satan to attempt to disrupt and corrupt the church at this critical juncture. He has a history of doing such things.

Even back in the book of Genesis, the deceiver himself sought to corrupt the sweetness of the blessings, intimacy, and unity felt between Adam and Eve and God in the garden, and he was able to do so through subtle temptation. So it makes perfect sense that the sin of temptation and deception would seek to undermine the spiritual momentum the church was experiencing in those early days. We see this come to fruition at the beginning of chapter 5.

> But a man named Ananias, with his wife Sapphira, sold a piece
> of property. However, he kept back part of the proceeds with his
> wife's knowledge, and brought a portion of it and laid it at the
> apostles' feet.
>
> Acts 5:1–2

On the surface one may ask, "What's the problem? Ananias and Sapphira owned the land in the first place. Don't they have the right to keep some of the profit for themselves?" Well, yes, but . . . they didn't tell people that's what they were doing. Instead, they led people to believe that this was the full proceeds of their sale. They wanted full credit for their sacrifice while pocketing some of the profit behind the scenes. In other words, they secretly wanted both the money and the public notoriety or praise.

This kind of deception and hypocrisy in order to achieve some kind of spiritual status or standing within the church was not going to be tolerated, and God gave Peter insight into what was really happening.

> "Ananias," Peter asked, "why has Satan filled your heart to lie to the Holy Spirit and keep back part of the proceeds of the land? Wasn't it yours while you possessed it? And after it was sold, wasn't it at your disposal? Why is it that you planned this thing in your heart? You have not lied to people but to God."
>
> Acts 5:3–4

A profound truth in our theology of the Holy Spirit is seen here. Peter says that in lying to the Holy Spirit, Ananias has lied to God. God knows, God sees, and God will judge.[1] If there was one thing that Christ found absolutely reprehensible in his ministry here on earth, it was the desire to seek spiritual fame and glory through hypocrisy, which is why the Pharisees and religious leaders in Israel were his greatest enemies.

At this critical juncture of the early church's infancy, God chose to "put the fear of God" in all of them by taking immediate judiciary action.

> When he heard these words, Ananias dropped dead, and a great fear came on all who heard. The young men got up, wrapped his body, carried him out, and buried him.
>
> Acts 5:5–6

Boom! Just like that. Judgment fell hard and fell quickly, and before you know it, Ananias was buried in the ground. Instead of public praise and some pocket change, he received a grave instead. But God was not finished yet. It was now his wife's turn to come clean, but she kept up with the charade.

> About three hours later, his wife came in, not knowing what had happened. "Tell me," Peter asked her, "did you sell the land for this price?"
>
> "Yes," she said, "for that price."

> Then Peter said to her, "Why did you agree to test the Spirit of the Lord? Look, the feet of those who have buried your husband are at the door, and they will carry you out." Instantly she dropped dead at his feet. When the young men came in, they found her dead, carried her out, and buried her beside her husband.
>
> Acts 5:7–10

Once again, instant judgment. Peter even gave her a chance to confess, with the implication that she may have been spared, but she continued to play the game. And three hours later, she lay in a grave next to her husband.

So why so harsh? Why is this in the Bible? The text gives us insight.

> Then great fear came on the whole church and on all who heard these things.
>
> Acts 5:11

We live in a time when many believers today are too casual and presumptuous with their sin. We figure that we are covered by grace and therefore we lose some of that "holy fear and trembling" before a holy God. But God is not meant to be mocked or taken advantage of, and this story stands as a reminder that sin is a horrific offense to his pure and spotless nature.

Sure, God's grace is abundant and never-ending. But it is not cheap grace, and in this case, God decided to call Ananias and Sapphira home and take them out of the game they were playing lest they corrupt the whole congregation. For as Paul elsewhere said, "A little yeast leavens the whole batch of dough" (1 Corinthians 5:6 NIV).

Further, this seminal time in the church was the perfect time for Satan to attempt to throw a wrench in the spokes in order to bring corruption and destruction to the blessings God intended for his people. But God was not about to allow that. He wanted the church firmly established, and this divine discipline served as a deterrent to anyone who sought to exploit the blessings of God for personal gain.

God is sovereign, and he can decide to bring one of his children home to heaven whenever he so chooses. Our lives ultimately belong to him. Each day that we live and each breath that we take are truly another moment of his grace. I am thankful he doesn't treat us as our sins deserve. But if he calls me home, I'd rather hear him say, "Well done" than "What were you thinking?"

So this story has a place in our Bibles: to show us how holy God is, how offensive our sin is to him, how important the church is in his sight, and how blessed we are when God chooses to be patient with us. The story may also have helped God establish Peter's leadership as an apostle who had insight into divine revelation received directly from God. Either way, the church learned a clear and valuable lesson, and God's power and might was once again exalted in their midst.

He is holy.

28

Handling Snakes and Drinking Poison

I t is widely held among New Testament scholars today that Mark 16:9–20 is not a part of the original gospel of Mark but was added by scribes in the second century who felt that the gospel ended too abruptly.[1] Here are some of the reasons for this conclusion:

1) The two oldest and most reliable Greek manuscripts of Mark do not include it.

2) The style, structure, and vocabulary of the Greek do not match the rest of the gospel of Mark, including up to eighteen words that Mark never used before. In fact, the transition between verse 8 and verse 9 is rather awkward, even seemingly introducing Mary Magdalene all over again when Mark had already talked about her in the previous chapter (15:40, 47).

3) The early church historian named Eusebius (c. 265–340 AD), along with the early church father Jerome (c. 340–420), who was the first to translate the Bible into Latin, state in their writings that of the earliest manuscripts that were known to them, none of them included verses 9–20.

4) Other early church theologians, including Clement, Origen, and Cyprian, show no knowledge that this additional ending even existed. Two theologians—Tatian (c. 120–180 AD) and Irenaeus (c.130–202 AD)—suggest the longer ending was composed in the second century and is not a part of Mark's original gospel, which he wrote likely somewhere in the late 50s AD.

5) Bible scholar James R. Edwards remarks, "The longer ending also includes themes particular to itself, some of which contradict Markan themes. The repeated chastisement of the disciples for their 'disbelief' of the gospel proclamation is unique to the longer ending, and the prominence given to the charismatic signs in verses 17–18 stands in stark contrast to the reserve of Jesus in Mark with regard to signs and sensation (cf. 8:11–13)."[2]

Though most (but not all) of the content of Mark 16: 9–20 can be corroborated elsewhere in the New Testament, the most unique and consequently the most controversial verses are 17 and 18.[3]

> "And these signs will accompany those who believe: In my name they will drive out demons; they will speak in new tongues; they will pick up snakes; if they should drink anything deadly, it will not harm them; they will lay hands on the sick, and they will get well."
>
> Mark 16:17–18

It is true that the disciples were uniquely equipped by Jesus to cast out demons and supernaturally heal (Mathew 10:1). The use of tongues (known human languages) was also present in the early church (Acts 2:4; 1 Corinthians 14). Still, nowhere in the Bible do we see Christ-followers purposefully picking up and handling snakes or drinking poison and other deadly substances as "signs of faith." The apostle Paul was bitten by a venomous snake (Acts 28:3–6) and was "spared any harm," but this was not common among the believers and is usually understood to be an apostolic miracle.[4]

Further, nowhere else in the Bible do we see believers drinking anything poisonous or deadly and surviving as a testament to their faith. This is not the kind of "fruit" or "evidence" of faith that the Bible aspires the church to display (and it is certainly not a part of the Great Commission of Matthew 28 or the fruit of the Spirit in Galatians 5).

Unfortunately, some fringe Pentecostal groups in the Appalachian Mountains and elsewhere have taken these verses to heart, implemented them quite literally, and have seen tragic consequences. In April 1973, the *New York Times* reported that in Tennessee a pastor and a congregational member from the Holiness Church of God in Jesus Name in Carson Springs both died as a result of drinking strychnine in an attempt to demonstrate their faith.[5]

More recently, in 2014, a Pentecostal pastor from the Full Gospel Tabernacle in Jesus Name in Middlesboro, Kentucky, died when a rattlesnake he was handling in a worship service bit him on the right hand. The pastor refused medical treatment and was dead several hours later. A local CBS news affiliate interviewed the pastor's son, who reportedly said, "The snake that bit him, we've been carrying him to the church for about four months. . . . It's been carried hundreds of times, handled all kinds of times but now when it's your time to go, it's just your time to go."[6]

It has been suggested that nearly 125 different churches in the United States still practice snake handling, and that this originated with the rise of the Holiness Pentecostal movement over a hundred years ago (though I would add that this is not normally a part of the majority of Pentecostal churches).[7] Though in most states it is against the law to practice this (one exception is West Virginia), there are certainly those that still do and risk their lives.

Apparently, those who practice this may feel that it is their way of testifying to their faith over and against the power of the devil. And if they die, they merely think that "their time is up." In the last century, over one hundred people have died in the hills of eastern Tennessee due to this dangerous practice.[8]

This is tantamount to "testing the Lord" in an unhealthy, unbiblical, and reckless manner. When Jesus was tempted by Satan in the wilderness, he quoted Deuteronomy 6:16 when he said, "You shall not put the Lord your God to the test" (Matthew 4:7 ESV). But snake handling and drinking poison are doing just that, as if one is wanting God to "prove himself" in his promise of Mark 16:18 as one daringly seeks to "validate" or "prove" one's faith.

I realize that handling snakes and drinking poison are extreme examples of people who are inappropriately testing God, but I would suggest to you that people do in fact put God to the test in different ways. Many use Gideon's bad example of putting out a fleece in an attempt to "put God on the hook" to reveal his will.[9] Others buy into what I call "foxhole Christianity," which is the idea that people will make dramatic promises to God in their time of trial "if only he would do this or that" and rescue them from distress.[10]

None of these are ways in which God intends our relationship with him to function. Putting God to the test is nothing short of demonstrating how *little faith* we have in light of what God has already promised us. Gideon already knew the will of God, but he was insecure and lacked faith and desired to put God to the test using a fleece. Though God was gracious with Gideon, this was certainly not meant to be a pattern in how to discern God's will. We should not be looking for subjective, external, unbiblical signs that we are tempted to read into in order to find God's will.

So when it comes to this alternative ending to the gospel of Mark (16:9–20), I would assert to you that it should probably not be in our Bibles, or at the very least, should be read carefully and critically and compared to the teachings of the rest of Scripture. I might go as far as suggesting that we should be cautious about regarding this as inspired Scripture. There is simply not enough internal or external evidence to verify that this was a part of the original manuscript of Mark, and its teachings can be widely misunderstood and misused.

Why then is it in there in the first place? Its presence in many late Greek manuscripts could be attributed to the fact that later scribes added it in order to fill in what they thought was missing from the story, a point I mentioned earlier.[11] Further, Erasmus, the Dutch philosopher and professor of Greek who taught in Cambridge, England, among other places in the early 1500s, was one of the first to produce and publish a fully Greek New Testament text, and the only manuscripts he had at his disposal included the longer ending to Mark.

It was his publication of the Greek text that became known as the *Textus Receptus*, the primary text translators of the King James Version used when translating the Greek into English in the early seventeenth century.[12] Therefore, due to the impact both the English Geneva Bible and the King James Version has had on Western Christianity, it became a tradition to include it in our Bibles. However, you might find in your Bible a statement in the margins or in the notes that says something along the lines of, "The most reliable manuscripts do not include Mark 16:9–20."

Either way, we have it, and though it is likely not a part of Mark's original gospel, we must still address it. I suggest we recognize the facts and ideas in it that are affirmed elsewhere in the gospel accounts and in the rest of the New Testament, like the "preaching of the gospel to all creation" (16:15) and the ascension of Christ (16:19). But we should not derive any teachings of the Christian faith on the basis of verses 9 to 20 alone.

So let's put down the snake and push away from the poison. That's not how we are to demonstrate our faith. Those ideas may, in fact, stem from a sneaky serpent, and that didn't end well for us.

29

The Battle for Moses' Body

DEUTERONOMY 34:1–8; JUDE 9

There are times when the Bible makes little "side comments" that may surprise or puzzle us. Out of nowhere comes unexpected information. This is especially true when the New Testament refers to something that happened hundreds of years earlier in the Old Testament. To be sure, the New Testament often clarifies and enriches our understanding of previous biblical history, shining more light and bringing greater focus as God reveals more to us.

One fascinating example is found in the book of Jude, which refers to Moses' death hundreds of years earlier and shows an unseen world that is not normally available for us to see or know about. It is the angelic world, which plays a special role in carrying out the plans and will of God. Some background context may be helpful.

Moses was a spiritual giant in Israel's history, a towering figure with a seemingly impossible task—to lead God's people out of bondage in Egypt at the hands of Pharaoh and into the land of

Canaan, or what we affectionately call the Promised Land. Moses encountered the LORD in a burning bush and was commanded to return to Egypt (where he was born and raised) to help deliver God's people from slavery and bondage. Equipped with God's blessing and power, he performed miracles and wonders before Pharaoh (ten devastating plagues), until finally the angel of the LORD spelled freedom from slavery as a result of the Passover miracle where the firstborn son of all Egyptians was lost during the judgment of God.

Pharaoh's grip on the Hebrew slaves finally was released, and Moses led them into the wilderness where God went ahead to guide them with a pillar of cloud by day and fire by night (Exodus 13:21). After changing his mind, Pharaoh then pursues the Israelites with his army until they are trapped against the Red Sea. In what is yet another major miracle, God instructs Moses to raise his staff, and the sea is parted so that the Israelites can cross on dry land.

Pharaoh, in hot pursuit with his armies, enters into the dry sea floor after the Israelites, and the LORD causes the waters to return, drowning and killing Pharaoh and all his army. As they head through the wilderness, the people of God begin to complain and rebel about food and water, and the LORD once again miraculously provides for them water, manna, and quail. They encounter and defeat the Amalekites in battle and arrive at Mount Sinai.

It is here at Sinai that they encounter the LORD and through Moses are given the laws of God that find their greatest expression in the Ten Commandments. The LORD makes a covenant with his people, but when Moses returns from the mountain, he finds the Israelites worshiping a golden calf. A plague ensues, and many are put to the sword or for their spiritual idolatry.

After leaving Mount Sinai, they proceed to the wilderness of Paran, where they send in spies to investigate the Promised Land. Ten of the twelve spies return with intimidating news, and the Israelites balk and decide not to enter. God's anger burns against them and he proclaims that this unbelieving generation of Israelites will not enter the land—except for Joshua and Caleb, the two spies who were willing to go in the first time. Even Moses and Aaron, who led the Israelites, would be disciplined for not honoring the Lord's holiness and following his commands when Moses inappropriately struck a rock in the quest for water (whereby the Lord had told them to *speak* to the rock instead; see Numbers 20). They too would not be allowed to enter the Promised Land.

After Aaron's death, Moses prepared to hand over the leadership reins to Joshua, who would be the one to lead them into the land. After a series of important speeches, Moses is told by the Lord to climb Mount Nebo, where he will show him all the land that Israel will inherit, though Moses himself will not enter into it. It is here that Moses will die at the age of 120.

What happens at his death is quite interesting and noteworthy. We pick it up in Deuteronomy 34 when he is up on the mountain looking into the land.

> The Lord then said to him, "This is the land I promised Abraham, Isaac, and Jacob, 'I will give it to your descendants.' I have let you see it with your own eyes, but you will not cross into it."
>
> So Moses the servant of the Lord died there in the land of Moab, according to the Lord's word. He buried him in the valley in the land of Moab facing Beth-peor, and no one to this day knows where his grave is.
>
> Deuteronomy 34:4–6

Did you notice the last sentence, verse 6? Moses died, and *the Lord buried him* in the valley where no one would know where the grave is. So the greatest of all Israel's prophets (Exodus 34:10) was buried by none other than God himself. The question is, Why would the Lord remove all others from being a part of Moses' burial?

Speculation abounds, but two likely reasons come to mind. One is that God wanted to protect the body of Moses from possible desecration by his enemies (in Israel and outside of Israel), or second, God knew about the propensity of the Israelites to worship idols and wanted to protect this servant of God from being put on a pedestal, so to speak.

With regard to the latter suggestion, Old Testament scholar Christopher Wright offers his insights:

> One interesting view is that the scriptures had to emphasize the human mortality of Moses in order to balance the emphasis through the Pentateuch (and especially in Deut.) on his closeness to God. There was a danger that one who had spent so much time face to face with God (v. 10), one who spoke for God almost interchangeably at times, one who had mediated the blessings and judgments of God, might come to be unduly venerated. Hence the stress on his mortality, supplemented by the note that since nobody knew where his grave was it could not become a distracting and potentially idolatrous shrine. Moses is not more and no less the servant of the LORD.[1]

I believe this latter suggestion holds significant weight. The human potential for idolatry, even to idolize Moses, one they often opposed, was strong in Israel. I have found this phenomenon to be true today, where in memorial services there is a tendency to venerate a loved one in such a way that one wonders if they had any imperfections at all. It is funny how our perceptions and opinions sometimes change after a loved one dies.

Nevertheless, the Israelites demonstrated little control over their urge to worship created things rather than the Creator, so God may have seen to it that this would not happen in this case.

Further evidence that this was why the LORD himself buried Moses is found in the book of Jude, where Jesus' half brother speaks about the bold and reckless arrogance of false teachers who slander angelic beings and reject authority. They seek to command spirits that they have no authority over. To illustrate why this is not appropriate, he uses a strange illustration.

> In the same way these people—relying on their dreams—defile their flesh, reject authority, and slander glorious ones. Yet when Michael the archangel was disputing with the devil in an argument about

Moses's body, he did not dare utter a slanderous condemnation against him but said, "The Lord rebuke you!"

Jude 1:8–9

Here is where we get insight into Moses' burial in a way that was not mentioned in the Old Testament. Apparently, the devil had an interest in the body of Moses, perhaps for the reason we mentioned earlier (idolatry), even though the reason is not explicitly stated here in Jude. To make sure the body of Moses stayed hidden and secure, the LORD apparently sent the archangel Michael to watch over the body and oppose the devil from taking hold of it and using it for some evil purpose.

One of the most powerful angels in the Bible, the archangel Michael, chose not to rebuke the devil (who himself is very powerful, perhaps even a fallen cherub—see Ezekiel 28:14) but instead said, "The LORD rebuke you!" Even in this battle, Michael chose not to address the devil; some suggest this is wise counsel even for us today—that we should put on the armor of God (Ephesians 6) instead of speaking and commanding celestial beings as if we were an apostle commissioned by Christ himself to do such things.

No matter where one stands on the latter discussion (as to whether we should be talking to the devil), it is clear from this text that in the angelic realm there was a fuss over the body of Moses. And God wanted to make sure that Moses was not exploited by the devil, so he buried him (perhaps even by using the archangel Michael to do it).

Fascinating. But why is this story in the Bible? I suggest it's there to remind us there is an unseen realm that is privy only to God (unless he chooses to reveal it like he does here). We have no idea what goes on in the heavenly realms, and this should humble us.

It also reminds us of the ways in which God protects us from the Evil One. The LORD protected Israel from even further idolatry and from the devil using the body for some evil purpose. When the tape of our own lives is played back, we might be surprised to see so many ways in which God protected us as well.[2]

30

Angel Armies

≡ 2 KINGS 6:8–23 ≡

A s I've said before, certain Bible stories just grab your soul. They are a feast for the imagination, stories where you say, "I wonder what *that* was like?" This next passage in 2 Kings is one of those. It features Elisha, the protégé of Elijah. They are considered two of the greatest miracle-working prophets in Israelite history. After Elijah is whisked to heaven, Elisha becomes the main "man of God" in Israel, and God's desire to protect his people from their enemies is on full display when he employs Elisha to help protect Israel in a rather unique way.

This story involves the nearby nation of Aram (Syria), led by their king, Ben-hadad II (who ruled c. 860–841 BC). The Arameans (Syrians) were essentially pests, always in conflict with Israel, often sending small bands of raiding parties who would plunder villages in Israel. They were not in all-out war all the time, but they were quickly heading in that direction. We pick up our story in 2 Kings 6.

When the king of Aram was waging war against Israel, he conferred with his servants, "My camp will be at such and such a place." But the man of God sent word to the king of Israel: "Be careful passing by this place, for the Arameans are going down there." Consequently, the king of Israel sent word to the place the man of God had told him about. The man of God repeatedly warned the king, so the king would be on his guard.

2 Kings 6:8–10

So the King of Aram gets together with his officers and basically says, "Let's plan a raid against the Israelites and set up camp somewhere over here." But the moment they do that, God shares the Aramean plan with Israel's prophet Elisha, and he subsequently warns the king of Israel to stay away.

This happens numerous times, such that the Arameans' plans to attack always end up being thwarted. Obviously this was frustrating for the king of Aram. You make your best plans, you strategize with your generals, and some prophet gets the memo from God and spills the beans.

The king of Aram was enraged because of this matter, and he called his servants and demanded of them, "Tell me, which one of us is for the king of Israel?" One of his servants said, "No one, my lord the king. Elisha, the prophet in Israel, tells the king of Israel even the words you speak in your bedroom."

2 King 6:11–12

The king is fuming. He thinks he has a traitor in his own camp, and he demands to know who it is. Then the truth comes out: Israel has a prophet, and he somehow knows the secret conversations that take place in the king's private quarters (a scary thought).

Clearly, nothing escapes God's attention, and the king of Aram is getting a firsthand lesson in this. But one thing we will quickly notice is that the king of Aram is not too bright. He learns nothing from this, and he once again plans a "secret" ambush—this time to capture Elisha with an even bigger army than before.

So the king said, "Go and see where he is, so I can send men to capture him." When he was told, "Elisha is in Dothan," he sent horses, chariots, and a massive army there. They went by night and surrounded the city.

2 Kings 6:13–14

This prompts an obvious question: Why does the king think this *new secret plan* will finally take Elisha by surprise? God told Elisha all the other plans, but somehow the king thinks he's going to handle the situation with this *new covert operation*. Don't you hate it when we make the same mistakes all over again? The heart of wisdom is one that learns from mistakes, but the king of Aram is not wise.

Surely Elisha knows about this plan too, but this time he allows it to happen because he knows God has bigger plans in the end. The Aramean army finds out where Elisha is, and they surround the city in the middle of the night, ready to snag Elisha in the morning. In their minds, they are finally going to put an end to this prophet who foils all their plans.

When the servant of the man of God got up early and went out, he discovered an army with horses and chariots surrounding the city. So he asked Elisha, "Oh, my master, what are we to do?"

2 Kings 6:15

Elisha's (unnamed) servant gets up the next morning and, "Whoa!" his eyes bulge. The Arameans have surrounded them.

I am sure you have felt like this before. You wake up one morning, you go outside, and it seems like the world is dead set against you. You feel surrounded, the cards are stacked against you, the pressure is on, and the only thing you can say is, "LORD, why are you doing this? Help me."

In these moments we can wallow in the mud, go completely negative, and try to figure things out on our own, or we can decide to trust that God has a plan we do not see.

What we are going to see is that while his servant is in a panic, Elisha is not. Why is that? Because the servant is seeing with human

166

eyes and Elisha is seeing with spiritual eyes. So the question for us today is this: Which set of eyes are we more accustomed to using? Do you see the world through earthly glasses most of the time, or are you looking at life through the lens of Scripture with faith and trust in God as the filter that colors everything?

The servant is in a panic when Elisha speaks,

> "Don't be afraid, for those who are with us outnumber those who are with them."
>
> 2 Kings 6:16

At this point, the servant is undoubtedly confused. What is Elisha talking about? From the servant's perspective, there are just two of them, and they are severely outnumbered. But what he didn't know was that they were surrounded by more than Arameans.

> Then Elisha prayed, "LORD, please open his eyes and let him see." So the LORD opened the servant's eyes, and he saw that the mountain was covered with horses and chariots of fire all around Elisha.
>
> 2 Kings 6:17

Notice what delivers the servant from the *human perspective, from human panic, and from human doubt and fear.* Look what changes everything. Verse 17 says, "Elisha prayed." The outward circumstances did not necessarily change, but the internal perspective did, all as a result of prayer. This is just one of the many ways God uses prayers. Sometimes he uses it as a means to change circumstances, but more often than not it is the means he uses to change us so that we see things from his perspective.

What those two men were seeing was nothing less than the angelic armies of the living God. Amazing. The mountains were full of angels. Chariots of fire! Friend, we have no earthly idea how many times God has sent his army out on our behalf to save us from so many seen and unseen things that Satan has thrown at us.

As believers, we are to *live by faith and not by sight* (2 Corinthians 5:7). We're told that *greater is he that is in us than he that*

167

is in the world (1 John 4:4). We have God on our side, and *if God is for us, who can be against us?* (Romans 8:31). No matter what happens, we must put our hope in God.

Contrary to what the servant may have felt, Elisha and his servant were about the safest people on the planet in that moment. One guy saw the armies of earth, and the other guy saw the armies of heaven. And when the prayer of faith was offered by a man of faith, both guys could see God's ultimate plan and the victory he had in store over the evil that surrounded them.

> When the Arameans came against him, Elisha prayed to the LORD, "Please strike this nation with blindness." So he struck them with blindness, according to Elisha's word. Then Elisha said to them, "This is not the way, and this is not the city. Follow me, and I will take you to the man you're looking for." And he led them to Samaria.
>
> 2 Kings 6:18–19

Now in Samaria, Israelite territory, they are completely at the mercy of the Israelite king.

> When they entered Samaria, Elisha said, "LORD, open these men's eyes and let them see." So the LORD opened their eyes, and they saw that they were in the middle of Samaria. When the king of Israel saw them, he said to Elisha, "Should I kill them, should I kill them, my father?"
>
> Elisha replied, "Don't kill them. Do you kill those you have captured with your sword or your bow? Set food and water in front of them so they can eat and drink and go to their master."
>
> 2 Kings 6:20–22

Elisha prays again, for the third time. Their eyes are reopened, and the Arameans realize they're surrounded and vulnerable. The Israelite king (Jehoram) wants to wipe them out and put them to death, but Elisha essentially says, "Nope, if you had captured them, you would not have put them to death in cold blood, so that's not going to happen here." Elisha orders the king to give the enemy food and water and send them back home in an act of kindness.

> So he prepared a big feast for them. When they had eaten and drunk, he sent them away, and they went to their master. The Aramean raiders did not come into Israel's land again.
>
> 2 Kings 6:23

Obviously, the plan to use the little bands of terrorists to raid Israel did not work because of Elisha. Godliness has a way of thwarting the attacks of the enemy, and this is why we too should put on the armor of God (Ephesians 6).

Why is this story in the Bible, other than the fact that it is even more historical testimony to God's glorious power and his sovereign plans for his people? I can think of many possible reasons, as God continually gave testimony to his saving hand through the powerful words of his prophets. At the practical level, here are some clear applications:

1. It is designed to teach us that God is always sovereignly in control of everything that pertains to our lives, and so we should trust him no matter the circumstances.
2. Prayer enables us to see things from God's perspective and is often the means that God uses to bring us victory over spiritual opposition. (See Ephesians 6:18.)
3. Prayer opens our eyes to see where God is at work so that we can see the spiritual side of normal, everyday events.

I cannot help but wonder about God's angel armies, sent as "ministering spirits" to those who "will inherit salvation" (Hebrews 1:14). When we walk in obedience to God, we can walk securely knowing that nothing happens to us that does not first come or pass through his sovereign hands. For the believer, God works all things together for good, and the greatest good for us is to make us more like his Son (Romans 8:28–29). Oh, that we might have eyes to see, so that we too might know that God is on our side.

31

Bodily Discharges

≡ LEVITICUS 15 ≡

Sometimes the Bible talks about "unmentionables"—private issues in life that can be uncomfortable to discuss. For example, although our culture has become much more explicit, there is still in many circles a reticence to talk about things that our bodies experience—things we are prone to cover up or keep to ourselves. But when the LORD set forth parameters for how to worship him in the old covenant age, he was not afraid to talk about the realities of life. But first, a little context.

When the Israelites were delivered by the LORD from their bondage in Egypt, they embarked on a journey that would define their identity as the chosen people of God for the rest of human history.[1] From the time that Jacob (renamed "Israel") went to Egypt to the giving of the law at Mount Sinai, 430 years had passed (cf. Exodus 12:40). The people knew nothing but Egypt.

But now, released from slavery, they tasted the LORD's miracles and encountered him in a dynamic way at Mount Sinai, making a covenant with him through Moses, their prophet and intermediary. From then on, God's presence would be with them in a dramatic way—first meeting Moses temporarily in the "tent of meeting" and then later in the tabernacle (which became the new "tent of meeting").[2]

The covenant laws were given to Moses and passed on to the people, and a system of worship that included feasts and festivals and appointed sacrifices was set in place, regulated by a priesthood led by a high priest. They were to learn a new way to worship the one true God, abandoning the pagan rituals and polytheistic "gods" of their former captors and the surrounding nations.

The LORD gave Israel no fewer than 613 laws, including civil, ceremonial, and moral laws. As those who were set apart to be a "holy nation" (Exodus 19:6), these laws would govern their daily life, shape their way of thinking, and be an expression of their faith.

The book of Leviticus is one of those widely misunderstood books of the Bible because it is giving specific commands and responsibilities to the Levites and priests who were charged with overseeing the public worship of the LORD. They were further charged with teaching the people how to live a holy life so that they maintain a healthy relationship with a holy God, a God whose glory is the outward manifestation of his holy character.[3]

These commands were given only to the nation of Israel (no other nation), and they were to be followed until the time the law was to be fulfilled and completed by the perfect life and final sacrifice of Jesus Christ. Their righteousness would always come by faith, but the expression of it was to be found in these laws until Christ's fully atoning work (his life, death, and resurrection) would set it aside. Only then would they operate under a new covenant inaugurated by the giving of the Holy Spirit at Pentecost.

Today, as Christians, we are "no longer under the law but are under grace" (Romans 6:14), meaning that our acceptance before God is not conditioned upon obeying a set of laws but is instead found by grace through faith in Christ. To be sure, *the moral laws of God never change*, because God in his moral character does not change.

When we look at the list of laws in the Old Testament, we must see them as a *temporary steward* of what it meant to live a righteous life *under the Law of Moses*. The civil and ceremonial laws were designed only for Israel at that time, yet the moral laws still have application for all, insofar as they teach us "principles" for moral living. Since the old covenant has been set aside, we no longer follow "the letter of the law" today, but these laws can still speak to us about the nature and character of our holy God.

One peculiar chapter in Leviticus (chapter 15) catches us by surprise, and like we mentioned earlier, may even cause us to blush a bit. It covers the rules and regulations governing bodily discharges of both men and women, ranging from a sexual disease (likely gonorrhea), to an emission of semen, to menstruation. To make matters even more interesting, it frequently uses the concept of "unclean" and "clean" that may cause some confusion.

When we read in the Bible that something is unclean, it does not necessarily equate to *sinful*. This is a very important point. Though we may talk of the need to be *cleansed* from our sins and unrighteousness (1 John 1:9), the Bible also uses the words *clean* and *unclean* in a different way, referring to what the Israelites would understand as preparedness for worship (in a ceremonial sense).

Leviticus 10:10 states: "You must distinguish between the holy and the common, and the clean and the unclean." Certain animals and foods were always unclean, and certain activities could make one clean or unclean, either permanently or temporarily (and to various degrees).[4] Skin infections, contact with a dead body, childbirth, mildew, and, of course, bodily discharges could all make someone temporarily unclean, and certain actions (washings, offerings, sacrifices, etc.) were prescribed by the priests in order to regain ritual purity.

Throughout Israel's history, people would often wash in a *mikveh*, a bath used to achieve ritual or ceremonial purity. Without this, a person was not physically prepared to come into the presence of a holy God for worship. The Jews also used it as an opportunity to make themselves spiritually prepared to enter his presence. The specific activities or washing required was based on the level of uncleanness. John Hartley explains:

> Whenever a person became unclean in the course of daily routine, that person had to pursue the prescribed rituals for becoming clean in order to live in the camp. In cases of mild uncleanness, a person had only to wait until evening (e.g. [Leviticus] 11:24, 31), i.e., the beginning of a new day. In cases of more intense uncleanness, a person had to bathe and wait until evening (Leviticus 11:25; 15:5–8). These purification rituals continually reminded the congregation that all who wished to come up to the sanctuary had to prepare themselves to enter holy ground. They might never presume to enter God's presence casually. By preparing themselves ritually, they were in a position to approach God's presence with confidence, expecting his acceptance of their worship.[5]

Leviticus 15 deals with bodily discharges that would make one unprepared for worship. This includes a sexual disease of some type (perhaps gonorrhea):

> Speak to the Israelites and tell them: When any man has a discharge from his member, he is unclean. This is uncleanness of his discharge: Whether his member secretes the discharge or retains it, he is unclean. All the days that his member secretes or retains anything because of his discharge, he is unclean. Any bed the man with the discharge lies on will be unclean, and any furniture he sits on will be unclean.

> Leviticus 15:2–4

It may also include sexual activity:

> When a man has an emission of semen, he is to bathe himself completely with water, and he will remain unclean until evening. Any clothing or leather on which there is an emission of semen is to be washed with water, and it will remain unclean until evening.

173

> If a man sleeps with a woman and has an emission of semen, both of them are to bathe with water, and they will remain unclean until evening.
>
> Leviticus 15:16–18

A woman's normal menstrual period may make her temporarily unclean as well.

> When a woman has a discharge, and it consists of blood from her body, she will be unclean because of her menstruation for seven days.
>
> Leviticus 15:19

With the exception of the first type of discharge, which may be a sexual disease incurred by sin and thus call for a sin offering and burnt offering, none of these bodily discharges were to be seen as inherently sinful or disgusting. Rather, they were normal matters over the course of life that would make one temporarily unclean with respect to ritual purity. But God considered their return to ritual purity important lest they die by defiling his tabernacle (Leviticus 15:31).[6] He wanted the Israelites to be set apart for him, fixed on the importance of worship, and eagerly looking forward to being in his presence.

Other reasons God may have required a period of waiting and actions needed to obtain ritual purity include:

1. He wanted to regulate certain things, such as "encouraging restraint in sexual behavior."[7]
2. He wanted the Israelites to take God's holiness seriously and their need to be sanctified and set apart as a priority, so that things like fertility rites and cult prostitution that were a part of the Canaanite pagan rituals would be even further away from their daily life.[8]

To be sure, these laws concerning purity put boundaries around certain behaviors and made people aware of the need to avoid serious sins. With respect to menstruation, this is healthy and normal, and it was actually something that was not as common as it is today. Why? Because in ancient Israel women married early, had large families, and were therefore pregnant frequently until menopause.

Further, Wenham suggests that only unmarried teenage girls had a relative frequency of menstruation, and since any man who would "sleep with a woman who was menstruating" would himself be unclean for a period of seven days (see Leviticus 15:24), it would serve as a deterrent from inappropriate sexual sin on the part of the males. He writes,

> The relative frequency of their periods and the contagiousness of the uncleanness associated with menstruation should have made any God-fearing young man wary of any physical contact with a girl he did not know well, for if he went to worship in an unclean condition, he was liable to God's judgment. In this way these regulations may have promoted restraint in relations between sexes and have acted as a brake on the passions of the young.[9]

God is all-knowing and all-wise, and though sex in marriage is portrayed as a beautiful expression of love in God's sight (see the Song of Songs), human beings have a tendency to make an idol out of it and abuse it, taking it out of its proper context. We are not under the laws of the Old Testament anymore, but we can still see some of the wisdom behind them for a people the LORD wanted to be holy and set apart for him.

Today, as Christians, living in the power of the Holy Spirit is the only way to curb the appetites of the flesh and live set apart for God. And when we fall short, there is grace. We repent, turn back to him, and press on to maturity. In this way, we see our bodies as a temple, and we can approach him in worship with a clear conscience, so that we may thoroughly enjoy his presence.

32

Resurrections at Christ's Death

MATTHEW 27:51–53

A pivotal moment in human history took place when the sinless Savior Jesus Christ was crucified for sin on a Roman cross. The Scriptures foretold of this moment hundreds of years before it actually happened (Isaiah 53). Even more, God had planned for the event before the foundations of the world began (Acts 2:22–24; Revelation 13:8). So when it came to fruition, there was a dramatic reaction both within heaven and on earth.

It is an incredulous thought: God becoming a man, leaving the place of eternal glory, only to willingly submit to the most horrific form of execution ever devised by man, all out of love for us. Though all four gospel accounts record it, Matthew captures additional details that are sometimes lost in all the commotion. He records a series of miracles that form a bookend to the miracles that took place at Jesus' birth.

In his commentary on the Gospel of Matthew, James Montgomery Boice summarizes the five miracles that took place at the moment of Jesus' crucifixion:[1]

1. The darkening of the sky between noon and three in the afternoon, when Jesus was on the cross;
2. The tearing of the veil of the temple from top to bottom when Jesus died;
3. The earthquake that opened many of the tombs near the place of crucifixion;
4. Followed by the resurrection of life of many holy people who had died;
5. The cry of the centurion who said of Jesus when he saw these things, "Surely he was the Son of God."

Boice remarks that the last miracle was perhaps the greatest of them all, since it involves a wholesale transformation of the human heart. We don't often realize that God is still doing miracles today in many ways, especially when a spiritually dead human heart (Ephesians 2:1) is made alive (Ephesians 2:5) by grace through faith (Ephesians 2:8–9).

Christians believe in a supernatural God who does supernatural things, so we are not surprised when the Bible records supernatural events that make us stand in awe and wonder. The darkening of the sky is itself a sign of judgment—both on the people who rejected and murdered him, and on Jesus himself who at this time was bearing the wrath of God poured out for our sin. Jesus felt the weight of this as he experienced a break in fellowship with the Father, and cried out, "My God, my God, why have you forsaken me?" (Matthew 27:46 ESV).

The tearing of the temple curtain was another sign. The temple curtain blocked the entrance to the "Most Holy Place" within the temple that was only for the high priest to enter once a year during the Day of Atonement. Its tearing (note: from top to bottom, meaning it was done by God above and not man below) meant that now because of Christ's death, we could all have access to God's presence through faith in the crucified and soon to be risen Messiah (cf. Hebrews 10:19–22).[2]

Earthquakes in Israel are not necessarily rare, especially near the Temple Mount since there is a geological fault there, but the timing of this one seems truly remarkable. It is as if earth itself was hemorrhaging over the thought of its Creator being slain.

But the fourth miracle truly captures our imagination and makes us wonder.

> The tombs also were opened. And many bodies of the saints who had fallen asleep were raised, and coming out of the tombs after his resurrection they went into the holy city and appeared to many.
>
> Matthew 27:52–53

What an extraordinary event. Scholars are often quick to point out that Matthew's account of this raises more questions than we could possibly answer. Tombs seemingly were opened, but were the people raised at his death, or later, after his resurrection?

Option 1 is that the tombs were opened as a result of the earthquake, and that many of these godly people were raised from the dead *at the moment* Jesus died. After all, Matthew's point seems to be that the other four miracles took place at that moment as well.

Option 2 suggests that the tombs were opened by the earthquake and remained open for three days, *but that the people did not rise from the dead and appear to the people until after Jesus' resurrection*. The text seems to imply this as well. In that case, the miracle of their resurrections is not tied to Jesus' death but rather to Jesus' resurrection.

The hard part here is that option 1 and option 2 are both possibilities. I tend to think they were raised *at the moment* of his death but didn't show up until later, because Matthew is recording the miracles that took place when Jesus "yielded up his spirit" (v. 50).

Still, there is yet another issue to contend with. With what kind of body were they raised? Was it a natural body that by nature would have to die again (much like Lazarus)? Or was it a resurrection to a glorified body that would later be "raptured" up to heaven? I lean toward a natural body that had to die again instead of an immortal glorified body, and here is why.

The apostle Paul tells us that Jesus' resurrection is the "firstfruits" of those who have fallen asleep (i.e., "died") in 1 Corinthians 15:20. In other words, in the context of 1 Corinthians, Paul is arguing that Jesus is the first man to be raised from the dead with the immortal, glorified body, i.e., the "firstfruits," or the very first fruit of the harvest.

If these people were raised at his death (option 1), they would not have had a glorified body since Jesus was to become the first one to have that kind of body three days later. Again, Matthew's point in option 1 seems to be that all these things took place at the moment of Jesus' death. People were raised from the dead when Jesus died, but they didn't appear to people in the city until after Jesus' resurrection. They wouldn't have an immortal, glorified body if they were raised before Jesus. They would need to die again (what a bummer) because they had a natural body.

But isn't it possible that they weren't raised until after Jesus was raised (option 2), and therefore they could have received an immortal, glorified resurrected body like Jesus' body? If that was the case, then they would either still be with us today (since they were immortal), *or* they would have had to somehow been "raptured" and taken up to heaven later much like Elijah in the Old Testament (cf. 2 King 2). But there is no mention of any kind of translation to heaven by anyone other than Jesus after his resurrection. I think that if others were taken to heaven in glorified bodies, we would have likely heard about that from some of the other New Testament writers.

I lean toward the idea that all of these resurrected saints from the past were raised from the dead the moment Jesus died, with natural bodies that had to die again. They appeared *after* Jesus' own resurrection (so as not to steal his thunder before Resurrection Day, so to speak). I admit there is plenty of room for debate

179

on this, but the question still remains—why is this phenomenon in the Bible?

I don't know for sure, but here are some speculative ideas. The death of Christ was a huge event, and Matthew was committed to recording the history of what took place exactly as it happened without necessarily explaining to us all the meanings of each of those miracles (though the Hebrews writer talks about the curtain as we mentioned earlier).

Perhaps the miracle of the saints' resurrections is there to give us a foretaste and pledge of the final resurrection that will take place for all believers at Jesus' second coming.[3] Perhaps all these miracles are meant to portray theological truths that Christians would come to understand later—such as the need to confess Jesus as the "Son of God" (per the centurion) or the privilege we now have to come to God directly (since the curtain was torn) now that the priestly ministry of sacrifices in the temple was made obsolete by the final sacrifice of Jesus Christ.[4]

What we do know is that these things are recorded as they happened, and the Holy Spirit designed to include them for our benefit so as to encourage us in our reflection on the impact of Christ's death. The purpose is not to imagine what it was like to meet a dead saint raised to life, but rather we marvel over God's power over life—a power put on supreme display in the life, death, and resurrection of our coming King, who will one day raise us from the dead as well.

33

Dismemberment of a Concubine

≡ JUDGES 19 ≡

Few stories in the Bible are as dark and gruesome as the events that happen in Judges 19. One could say that this was one of the lowest points in all of Israel's history. We have covered some of the depravity that existed in Israel during the period of the judges, but nothing is as bad as what we see in this chapter.

Here we see the absolute worst of what the human heart is capable of due to the horrifying illness known as sin. At this point in the book of Judges, Israel has hit the bottom. Their sins have torn them away from the covenant blessings that were intended for them, and this story is nothing less than a physical manifestation of that reality.

In this period of the judges, Israel's pattern was to compromise its convictions, abandon its obedience to God, and fall into judgment. God would then remove his hand of protection and they would fall into the hands of their enemies, who would oppress them. Eventually, they would sober up, cry out to God, and he would hear their prayers. God would then raise up a deliverer, conquer their enemies, and they would *temporarily* return to God.

But in what seems to be five minutes later, they are right back into disobedience and idolatry. And as the cycles continue through the book of Judges, Israel's depravity seemingly gets worse. They continually allow themselves to be tainted by the surrounding Canaanite cultures. Even Israel's spiritual leadership was corrupt, to the very core.

The story of Judges 19 involves a Levite—a man from God's chosen tribe of priests—and a concubine, who had an unknown "falling out," causing her to leave him and return to her home.[1] After a period of four months, the Levite sets out to persuade his concubine to return to him, taking along a servant and two donkeys. Upon reaching the woman's home, the Levite is greeted warmly by the girl's father and is persuaded to stay for several days, so it wasn't until late in the fifth day that the Levite and company are able to leave, taking along the girl.

Refusing to stop in the foreign city of Jebus (later to become Jerusalem under David's reign) for the night, the Levite and his party travel on to Gibeah, a city belonging to the Israelite tribe of Benjamin. But unlike the girl's father, the Benjamites do not welcome them or practice hospitality. Though it would have been appropriate and expected in that culture, no one invites them into their home to shelter them for the night. It isn't until an old man from the hill country comes in from the fields and encounters them in the square that they are finally invited to stay in someone's home.

During the evening, while the visitors are being refreshed by eating and drinking at the old man's house, the wicked men of the tribe of Benjamin surround the house, pound on the door, and demand that the visitor (the Levite) be turned over to them so that they may have homosexual relations with him. The old man pleads with them to refrain from this vile behavior, and instead offers his virgin daughter and the Levite's concubine as a substitute for their sexual urges. Ironically, what the old man proposes is just as disgraceful and vile.

When the perverse men refuse to acknowledge or listen to his offer, the Levite drags his concubine outside to the "hungry" men who concede, and then rape and abuse the girl all through the night. Instead of protecting her and standing up to these men, this "priest" of God treats the girl with total shame and disgust, and then he heads off to bed. Meanwhile, unimaginable things happen to this girl as the men carry out their "unrestrained animal lust and human depravity."[2]

The next morning, the Levite gets ready to be on his way when he opens the door of the house only to find his concubine lying at the doorway. He demands that she get up, but there is no reply. The Levite then picks her up, throws her on his donkey, and takes her home. Horrifically, the priest proceeds to dismember the girl with a knife, cutting her into twelve pieces. The body parts are then sent throughout all Israel with a call to observe and respond to this outrage. All Israel is shocked by this grotesque and sickening display of human depravity, and a devastating civil war ensues to the point that the tribe of Benjamin is nearly completely destroyed.

The plot to this story is quite complex and reveals a multitude of sinful behavior. Amazingly, it parallels in many ways an earlier story in Genesis 19, where the sins of Sodom and Gomorrah are played out in similar fashion.

So the question remains: Why is this in the Bible? What are we to glean from this? First, the text itself tells us why it is in there.

> When he entered his house, he picked up a knife, took hold of his concubine, cut her into twelve pieces, limb by limb, and then sent her throughout the territory of Israel. Everyone who saw it said, "Nothing like this has ever happened or has been seen since the day the Israelites came out of the land of Egypt until now. *Think it over, discuss it, and speak up!*"
>
> Judges 19:29–30, emphasis mine

183

The news of this was a call to sober themselves up to the sin they were saturated in. Think, discuss, and speak up! It's time to repent! If this didn't shake them out of their sinful stupor, what would?

Second, the Bible doesn't sugarcoat reality. The reason these kinds of things are recorded in Scripture is that they serve as a warning to us.[3] Apart from God's transforming grace, we are totally depraved with a heart that is desperately wicked (Jeremiah 17:9). Most of us are not as bad as we could be, but the potential is there, and without God's saving power to change us, our sin has a way of destroying us. It is a pathway to death. As Paul has said, "The wages of sin is death" (Romans 6:23).

One must be very careful here. The Bible is not prescribing, endorsing, or advocating the kind of sinful behavior described in this passage, whether it be the taking of a concubine, homosexual relations, rape, or murder. It is merely *describing* what was happening, not *prescribing* it.

Unfortunately, these are the kinds of things that end up being taken out of context, misconstrued, and misunderstood. One should seek to understand what the book of Judges is intending to portray—a nation of Israel that has lost its way, rejecting authority, and doing that which is right in its own eyes (Judges 17:6).

The fact that this is even in the Bible argues for its authenticity, because if Israel was going to paint its history in a positive light to the world, they surely would not have wanted to include stories like this. But one thing is for sure. In order to understand the glorious wonder of God's love and miraculous grace, we have to understand what that grace is actually saving us from.

Grace saves us from the wrath of God that is due to sins like this. Even the vilest acts of our sinful nature can be forgiven if we repent of it and believe in the saving power of Christ to save us. Yes, it was for sin that he went to the cross, for the little white lie as well as the darkness of Judges 19.

This is why this is in the Bible—to show us our sin, so that we can see the glory of his grace.

34

Head Coverings

key principle to interpret the Bible properly is learning how to step inside the world and the time in which it was written—to "time travel," you might say. This is how you discover past culture and customs that might be altogether different from yours. The food, traditions, language, customs, and expectations would likely seem foreign to you, and there would be much that you would need to understand.

Context is key to biblical interpretation. And the context in which the apostle Paul wrote to the church in Corinth in the early-to mid-50s AD is important to understand.

Corinth was a key city along the Peloponnesian peninsula in southern Greece. Built at the foot of a mountain, it boasted a natural spring that flowed into town. This was important because fresh water was as good as gold in that day. Corinth was known for its seaport, and the fact that it stood on an isthmus that was bordered by the ocean on both sides made it a major trade route. Many ships would be put on skids and carried on rollers (portaged) across the isthmus to the ocean on the other side in order to avoid the long and dangerous trek around the southern end of the peninsula that was some 250 miles.

Corinth was a wealthy city, and though it was destroyed in a war in 146 BC, it was rebuilt and founded as a Roman colony a hundred years later. By the time of Paul, this city, some forty-five miles west of Athens, was a hub for Greek culture. It was known for its bronze art, architecture, and gross immorality. A temple to the god Apollo stood in the center of town, and other smaller temples for other "gods" were strung throughout the city.

Bathhouses, temple prostitutes, and other resources for plea-sure were common in this pagan culture. A temple to Aphrodite, the goddess of love, stood at the top of the mountain (known as the Acrocorinth) that overlooked the city. It is said that nearly one thousand temple prostitutes ("priestesses") were there, and they would often come down from the mountain to "serve the men" of the city, especially during the Isthmian Games, an athletic com-petition comparable to the Olympic Games, when lots of foreign visitors would be in town. Clearly, Corinth was a party city, and its debauchery and depravity were widely known.

There was a Jewish synagogue there, and most of the Jews rejected Paul's message. But the leader of the synagogue, Crispus, was converted to Christ along with his family, when Paul, along with his friends Priscilla and Aquila, shared the gospel during his second missionary journey. Soon others came to Christ as well, and the church in Corinth became a reality and began to grow.

Though many Christians in Corinth had been delivered from the immoral lifestyles they once participated in, they were still constantly tempted to fall back into old habits. Paul had spent eighteen months there (Acts 18:11) teaching God's Word, but the church evolved into a rather immature, fractured, and worldly church. Arrogance, selfish-ness, and sexual immorality were commonplace, and the social elites often stood apart from those less well off in the church.

This general lack of holiness and social disorder meant that worship services were anything but. Therefore, Paul gave much instruction in a letter concerning how worship was to be conducted in a way that would glorify God. His pastoral heart and love for the church is evident even in the midst of firm correction, and a mature combination of rebuke and encouragement pervades this letter.

In his letter, Paul addressed many issues concerning worship—the use of spiritual gifts, the Lord's Supper, and, curiously to many today, head coverings. He did this by first affirming the church and then laying down this basic Christian principle about the way men and women are to relate to each other: Instead of seeing women as merely sexual objects, like much of the Greek culture did, Christianity actually elevates women to a higher state of dignity as those who are equally created in the image of God. But even though women are equal in essence, worth, and abilities, there is still a *functional* order that God has established within marriage relationships, which is reflective of the way relationships *function* even within the triune Godhead.

> Now I commend you because you remember me in everything and maintain the traditions even as I delivered them to you. But I want you to understand that the head of every man is Christ, the head of a wife is her husband, and the head of Christ is God.[1]
>
> 1 Corinthians 11:2–3 ESV

Within the relationships mentioned here, there is an authority structure.[2] Again, this is so that the relationships mentioned can function properly, and is not to be seen as a power structure to be inappropriately used for selfish purposes. Even within the Godhead, God the Father and God the Son are equal in essence, deity, and importance (one God, three persons), but there is still a way in which their relationship functions in love. Certainly we see that played out in the Gospels as Jesus willingly submitted himself to the will of the Father.

Within the structure, the role of the husband is to serve as the functional spiritual leader of the wife, who is charged with submitting to his healthy, godly leadership (see Ephesians 5:22–33;

Colossians 3:18–19; 1 Peter 3:1–7).[3] John MacArthur makes a helpful comment:

> But he makes no distinction between men and women as far as personal worth, abilities, intellect, or spirituality are concerned. Both as human beings and as Christians, women in general are completely equal to men spiritually. Some women are obviously superior to some men in abilities, intellect, maturity, and spirituality. God established the principle of male authority and female subordination for the purpose of order and complementation, not on the basis of any innate superiority in males.[4]

How this structure plays out in the home and in the church is still debated with fervor today, but Paul made it clear how it was to be visualized and demonstrated in the first-century context of the Corinthian church. In that particular culture, a woman who was married signified that she was under the authority of her husband by wearing a head covering whenever she was in public, especially in the context of the church.

To go without the covering would have brought shame to the husband. And with regard to the husband, the reverse would be true. He was not to have his head covered. This is why Paul wrote this to the Corinthian church:

> Every man who prays or prophesies with his head covered dishonors his head, but every wife who prays or prophesies with her head uncovered dishonors her head, since it is the same as if her head were shaven. For if a wife will not cover her head, then she should cut her hair short. But since it is disgraceful for a wife to cut off her hair or shave her head, let her cover her head. For a man ought not to cover his head, since he is the image and glory of God, but woman is the glory of man. For man was not made from woman, but woman from man. Neither was man created for woman, but woman for man. That is why a wife ought to have a symbol of authority on her head, because of the angels. Nevertheless, in the Lord woman is not independent of man nor man of woman; for as woman was made from man, so man is now born of woman.

And all things are from God. Judge for yourselves: is it proper for a wife to pray to God with her head uncovered? Does not nature itself teach you that if a man wears long hair it is a disgrace for him, but if a woman has long hair, it is her glory? For her hair is given to her for a covering. If anyone is inclined to be contentious, we have no such practice, nor do the churches of God.

1 Corinthians 11:4–16 ESV

Since we are limited by what we can cover in this passage, we must stick with the task at hand. What Paul means by prophesying; the ways in which prostitutes in Paul's day shaved their heads; the woman being created for the "glory of man"; and even the presence of angels in worship are all subjects for another day. Here and now, the issue is head coverings.

For a woman to have her head uncovered in public was a sign that she was available to a man, either referring to something sexual or simply as an expression of being unmarried. But a married woman was to wear a head covering to show that she was unavailable and "under the authority" of her husband.

Further, the husband was *not* to wear a head covering, nor was he to have long hair, which in this day and age was seen as something that was naturally designed to accentuate a woman's beauty. All of these commands are contextual to that day's culture and ought not to be seen as binding on us today. What Paul is doing here is simply taking the timeless principle of male headship and female submission and *applying it to the context of the Corinthian church*.

The timeless principle is seen in verse 3 (head of Christ is God, the head of every man is Christ, and the head of the wife is her husband), since those ideas are rooted in the Godhead and the human relationships that reflect it. But the *working out of those timeless principles* is context-specific to the culture at hand with reference to external things like appearance and dress.

Today, Christians in North America are not bound to the specific way that Paul applied the overarching principle to the church in Corinth. We are charged with working out that principle in our own context (with regard to appearance and dress). Unfortunately, even today the latter issue of appearance and dress is still up for grabs in some circles. How one might look in certain parts of the country may even be different.

But in general, applying Paul's principle takes discernment, wisdom, and sensitivity to implement no matter what culture one finds oneself in. We must understand that the church has to grasp the basic principle before it can figure out how to apply it concerning external matters of everyday living.

Why is this in the Bible? It shows us that it is important for Christians to be faithful to God's ordained order for relationships (lest things crumble *functionally* speaking), and it reminds us that Christians need to use discernment when *implementing* timeless principles in whatever time and culture they find themselves. We are not to be like the world, but on nonessential matters of the faith we have freedom as well. The task of learning how to live "set apart" from the world while still having freedom from legalistic demands on external things will always be a challenge for us.

The culture of Paul's day would have required married women to wear head coverings, but our culture today would not. Hair was a big deal back then, and the *ESV Study Bible* gives a helpful footnote that summarizes our modern-day task:

> Although the norms of appropriate hair style (and dress) may vary from culture to culture, Paul's point is that men should look like men in that culture, and women should look like women in that culture, rather than seeking to disparage or deny the God-given differences between the sexes.[5]

Authority, submission, differences between men and women—it all reeks of controversy today. But the Bible does not leave us without principles to live by. The big task is to extract the timeless principle and to figure out how to implement it in our time. So let us proceed wisely, full of grace, with a desire to honor the Lord and his will.

35

"Eat My Flesh and Drink My Blood"

═ JOHN 6:53 ═

W ere the early Christians cannibals? It's a strange question, but some thought so. In Roman circles, the early Christians were the ones who were allegedly "eating the flesh" and "drinking the blood" of some hero named Jesus. To be sure, there were all kinds of rumors and speculations about the early Christians, ranging from cannibalism to incest (they called each other "brothers and sisters" and professed love for each other), and even atheism (they rejected the plural Roman gods and believed in an invisible one).[1]

None of them were true, obviously, but those on the outside who had little context for understanding the worldview of the Christian faith were quite puzzled and succumbed to ignorant speculation and rumors of the cruelest kind. But even for Jesus' followers, the sayings of Jesus were oftentimes hard to sort out and make sense of. Frankly, nobody talked like Jesus did. His words were filled with power, were poignant, and full of meaning.

So in the gospel of John, Jesus uses metaphorical speech in order to communicate a spiritual truth regarding his identity as the Messiah, calling himself the "bread of life" (John 6:35). Earlier in John 6, Jesus performed one of his most significant miracles in the feeding of the five thousand (upwards of twenty thousand if women and children were counted). Jesus' miracle was multiplying five loaves of barley and two fish in order to feed the multitude, something the Creator of the world (John 1:3; Colossians 1:16; Hebrews 1:2) is capable of doing.

Instantly, the people remembered the prophecy of Moses (the one who was their prophet when God fed them manna in the wilderness), who told them that one day, "The LORD your God will raise up a prophet like me from among you, from your countrymen, you shall listen to him" (Deuteronomy 18:15 NASB). Even Peter, later in Acts 3:23–24, would make this same connection between Moses' prophecy and Jesus.

Jesus was the man—the one Moses spoke about. His miraculous feeding along the Sea of Galilee triggered the hope of a messianic king who could once again deliver them from the tyranny of foreign rulers (this time Rome instead of Egypt), and the people immediately sought to make Jesus into their king, wishing him to be a militaristic messiah with political aspirations of delivering the Jews.

But his mission in his first coming was not about overthrowing an evil empire (that will come at his second coming). Rather, his mission this time was spiritual in nature, to meet the greatest need of God's people. His mission was about becoming the sacrifice for sin, and the offering of his body toward a substitutionary, sacrificial, and atoning death on a cross was to be the means of spiritual deliverance from the bondage of sin and death. Political and physical deliverance would have to wait.

Sensing their desire to make him king by force (John 6:15), Jesus withdrew to the mountainside to pray, and sent his disciples to get into a boat and head back to the other side of the sea, toward Capernaum. In what is yet another miracle, Jesus rescues the men who are caught in a storm in the middle of the night by walking on water to join them, and together they instantly arrive safely to the shore.

The next day the crowd finds Jesus, motivated by their desire for more food. But Jesus sees through their materialistic and superficial hungers and challenges them to hunger for more spiritual things, like eternal life, which he alone can offer. He then invites them to believe in him, but the people do not have an appetite for that. They would rather see more "bread from heaven" like the day before.

It is here that Jesus says, "I am the bread of life" (6:35). Yet they can only comprehend this materialistically, while Jesus is speaking metaphorically about spiritual realities.

> "I am the bread of life; whoever *comes* to me shall not hunger, and whoever *believes* in me shall never thirst."
>
> John 6:35 ESV, emphasis mine

Notice the key ideas involve "coming to" him and "believing" in him. This was not something they were willing to do (v. 36) or capable of doing without God's miraculous work of grace (vv. 37, 44). Their hearts were hardened because of sin. And as Jesus continues to press the metaphor of him being the "bread from heaven," he tells them that the bread he offers is "his flesh" (meaning he will offer up his body toward death on the cross).

Belief in him and in his impending substitutionary and sacrificial death on the cross will be the only thing that can nourish them spiritually, the only way they can experience the true "bread from heaven," which will grant them life forever (v. 51). But still, they struggle to understand, even arguing with each other in verse 52 about how Jesus was going to give "his flesh" for them to eat (missing the metaphor).[2]

So Jesus takes it a step further, adding to the metaphor, making it even more graphic.

So Jesus said to them, "Truly I tell you, unless you eat the flesh of the Son of Man and drink his blood, you do not have life in yourselves. The one who eats my flesh and drinks my blood has eternal life, and I will raise him up on the last day, because my flesh is true food and my blood is true drink. The one who eats my flesh and drinks my blood remains in me, and I in him. Just as the living Father sent me and I live because of the Father, so the one who feeds on me will live because of me. This is the bread that came down from heaven; it is not like the manna your ancestors ate—and they died. The one who eats this bread will live forever."

John 6:53–58

Without understanding the context of the metaphor then, this Scripture on the surface sounds rather gross. But putting it in the wider context is key to understanding its true meaning. To "eat his flesh" and "drink his blood" is tantamount to saying in a figurative sense that one must believe (v. 35) in the Messiah who will offer up his body and shed his blood on the cross for sin, one who will give his life "as a ransom for many" (Mark 10:45).

Only the person who possesses true saving faith in Jesus' life, death, and subsequent resurrection from the dead will receive eternal life. And the "flesh and blood" motif is the centerpiece of his saving work, showcased at the cross.

Some may try to see some overtones of the Christian celebration of the Lord's Supper, the Eucharist, or Communion in these verses. It is certainly true that when we eat the bread and drink the cup we are celebrating in a symbolic sense Jesus' death, an ordinance that Jesus instituted at the Last Supper with his disciples.

But I would caution you not to press that concept too far into these verses. The reason is, if you look closely at what Jesus said in verse 54, you will see that he makes a pretty significant promise. He promises that *"the one who eats my flesh and drinks my blood has eternal life, and I will raise him up on the last day."* If Jesus was referring to the communion service here (which he is not), then it would mean that whoever partook of the communion service in church was guaranteed eternal life and resurrection.

But yet this is not consistent with the overall teaching of Scripture that suggests that we are saved by grace through faith alone. I am a firm believer that only true believers should participate in a communion service. But since that does not always happen, I don't want unbelievers who do share in it to have some kind of false assurance that they are saved as long as they partake of the bread and the cup in church. So it is best to see Jesus' words as referring to a charge for us to have saving faith in his broken body and shed blood that was offered up for us at the cross.

Why are these strange sayings in the Bible? Why did Jesus talk about eating flesh and drinking blood? Perhaps it was to shock his listeners into understanding the true graphic nature of crucifying the Son of God. Or better yet, it helped separate those who truly believed from those who were there only for superficial and material nourishment. It is one of the "hard sayings" of Jesus, and it served its purpose, for later we are told that "from that moment many of his disciples turned back and no longer accompanied him" (John 6:66).

36

Saul, a Medium-Spiritist, and the Spirit of Samuel

≡ 1 SAMUEL 28 ≡

King Saul is a tragic figure in the history of Israel. The nation's first king, he was crowned due to Israel's unquenchable thirst to be like the surrounding nations who had kings of their own. This was never the ideal, as Israel was designed to be ruled by God alone through his word as ministered through his prophets and priests. But Israel had rejected that plan, and God in his sovereignty gave them a very spiritually weak king as a result of Israel's insistence (cf.1 Samuel 8).

Saul was tall, handsome, and full of pride. Though his reign got off on the right foot, missteps and continual disobedience to the LORD eventually disqualified him from having God's favor and blessing. His sins were rather bold. He inappropriately assumed priestly duties (1 Samuel 13:9–14), failed to destroy the enemies of Israel that the LORD had commanded him to destroy, and was even guilty of lying to the prophet Samuel.

As a result, the LORD decided to anoint David as the next king. He would have a troubled relationship with Saul, but he would not assume the role of king until some fifteen years later. Meanwhile, Saul's life and rule as king would continue on, but the unique empowerment of the Spirit of God to guide him as king was removed. In fact, an evil spirit would end up torturing Saul and causing him great distress the rest of his life.

Toward the end of his reign, in an act of desperation due to an impending war with the Philistines, Saul did something extremely unusual and extremely forbidden—he consulted a medium. The practices of divination, fortune-telling, sorcery, or seeking to consult the dead through a medium or necromancer were outlawed and condemned as evil in Deuteronomy 18, as they were occult practices of the surrounding Canaanites and were demonic in nature. Consulting the dead was not possible anyways since they are in an abode that is inaccessible to humans on earth.

When someone calls upon the dead, the medium essentially summons demons who imitate the spirits of the dead; this convinces the one who is summoning that they are really talking to them, and the "guidance" they get is essentially demonic in nature.

The actual punishment for being a medium or necromancer was stoning, according to the law of Moses (Leviticus 20:27). But Saul had done the right thing earlier when he kicked out all the mediums and necromancers from the land of Israel, emptying it of these wicked people (1 Samuel 28:3, 9).

But the usual ways of hearing from the LORD were not working for Saul (and this was because the LORD had rejected him as king and stopped listening to his prayers because of his disobedient sin—1 Samuel 15:23). Saul was desperate to hear something, so he disguised himself, left the land of Israel, and went into Philistine territory and consulted a medium in order to attempt to consult the spirit of the prophet Samuel (who was dead).

Saul disguised himself by putting on different clothes and set out with two of his men. They came to the woman at night, and Saul

said, "Consult a spirit for me. Bring up for me the one I tell you."
But the woman said to him, "You surely know what Saul has done,
how he has cut off the mediums and spiritists from the land. Why
are you setting a trap for me to get me killed?"

Then Saul swore to her by the LORD: "As surely as the LORD
lives, no punishment will come to you from this." "Who is it that
you want me to bring up for you?" the woman asked. "Bring up
Samuel for me," he answered.

1 Samuel 28:8–11

Interestingly, the woman herself was hesitant to perform her
trade because she feared being caught due to Saul's own decision
to cast mediums out of the land. Practicing it again would only
put her life in danger, and rightly so. What she didn't realize was
that the man asking was none other than the king of Israel himself.
How crazy is that? Surely Saul has stooped to his lowest of lows.

Saul assured her through an oath that she would not be punished for this, and she concedes and asks which dead person Saul
was interested in talking to. His response is quick: "Bring up Samuel." There was no one Saul trusted more than Samuel, the mighty
prophet and priest of Israel who had recently died (1 Samuel 28:3).

What is truly an amazing miracle and an unbelievable exception to the rule is that the LORD in his sovereign power *did not
allow any demon to imitate and speak on behalf of Samuel*, but
he allowed the actual spirit of Samuel to be consulted in order to
communicate to Saul his impending doom. The woman was initially horrified when she saw him. We are not sure why, but maybe
it was because he was not a demon but rather a perfectly holy man
(something that would have intimidated her).

When the woman saw Samuel, she screamed, and then she asked
Saul, "Why did you deceive me? You are Saul!" But the king said
to her, "Don't be afraid. What do you see?" "I see a spirit form
coming up out of the earth," the woman answered.

Then Saul asked her, "What does he look like?" "An old man is
coming up," she replied. "He's wearing a robe." Then Saul knew

that it was Samuel, and he knelt low with his face to the ground
and paid homage.

1 Samuel 28:12–14

Apparently, the LORD even allowed Samuel to be seen at an age
and dressed in a way that would be easily identifiable to Saul. Saul
knew who it was immediately and was gripped with reverence and
fear. I can't help but wonder if Saul himself was surprised this was
actually working—that the LORD would actually hijack a demonic
practice, override it, and use it to speak into Saul's life. Either way,
a dramatic encounter would ensue.

> "Why have you disturbed me by bringing me up?" Samuel asked
> Saul. "I'm in serious trouble," replied Saul. "The Philistines are
> fighting against me and God has turned away from me. He doesn't
> answer me anymore, either through the prophets or in dreams. So
> I've called on you to tell me what I should do."

1 Samuel 28:15

Saul's desperation is heard in his reply: "I'm in serious trouble."
Talk about an understatement. Little did he know that this was
all happening the night before he would be put to death by the
Philistines. He had reason to fear them, but ironically he feared
God less. Old Testament scholar Bill Arnold remarks,

> The matter-of-fact tone Saul uses seems to imply that he and
> Samuel can return to the early years of Saul's kingdom. Saul is
> hoping to turn back the clock to better days. It is as though he
> wants Samuel to forget all that has happened—as if he is saying
> "Please ignore this medium standing here and the illicit way I have
> contacted you, or your various condemnations of my character
> in the past, or the way I have recklessly sought to kill David while
> neglecting the Philistines all these years. Please tell me what to
> do now."[1]

But Samuel is not going to give Saul any advice on what to do with
the Philistines. Instead, he's going to remind him of the judgment

199

God has brought on him and *will* bring on him in the next twenty-four hours.

> Samuel answered, "Since the LORD has turned away from you and has become your enemy, why are you asking me? The LORD has done exactly what he said through me: The LORD has torn the kingship out of your hand and given it to your neighbor David. You did not obey the LORD and did not carry out his burning anger against Amalek; therefore the LORD has done this to you today. The LORD will also hand Israel over to the Philistines along with you. Tomorrow you and your sons will be with me, and the LORD will hand Israel's army over to the Philistines."
>
> 1 Samuel 28:16–19

Samuel announces Saul's doom. He is as good as dead. In fact, he even goes as far as to tell him that tomorrow will be his last day on earth, and then he and his sons will be dead. (The Philistines will kill his sons, and Saul will be wounded and will fall on his own sword in suicide.)[2] Saul practically faints to the ground, in utter terror. He is physically weak (he hasn't eaten all day). The woman feeds him, and he leaves, but his fate is sealed.

First Samuel 31 spells out the death of Saul and his sons. It is a grisly tale as they are routed by the Philistines who will find Saul dead by his own hand and will cut off his head much like David did when he cut off the head of the Philistine giant Goliath. They hung Saul's armor in their pagan temple and fastened his body, along with his sons, on a wall in a nearby city. Eventually, the bodies would be removed by some loyal locals who would take the desecrated bodies of Saul and his sons and would burn them, burying the bones so the bodies could not be humiliated anymore.

This story is nothing less than a horrific climax to a promising king whose disappointing life has met its darkest hour. Though the text does not explicitly say it, we are left with the impression that Saul's consultation of a medium was truly his last straw. His time was up. His sins had reached their limit, and the judgment of God fell hard and fast. In the end, Saul sought out what he initially rejected. Arnold explains:

> Saul turns to the illegitimate use of magic as a means of seeking guidance while closing his eyes to the prophetic word. The result, ironically, is that the magic he uses actually confirms the prophetic word he has scorned. Samuel's speech (28:16–19) makes this clear.[3]

If only Saul had listened and obeyed the voice of the LORD in the first place, perhaps it wouldn't have ended this way. And so this story in the Bible gives us a clear warning: Avoid demonic occult practices, but also heed the word of God so that blessing can follow obedience.

For even as Samuel had told Saul earlier, "To obey is better than sacrifice" (1 Samuel 15:22). But Saul wouldn't listen until it was too late. We will save ourselves much grief if we heed the word of God today, right now.

Though it is truly a biblical anomaly, we are stunned by the fact that God would choose to hijack an evil practice (consulting a medium) and use it in a completely unexpected way. Only he has the right, the authority, and the sovereign power to do such a thing. We are forbidden to consult or get anywhere near such a demonic practice. However, God is not culpable or wrong for breaking in or overriding it. He has a way of circumventing the evil actions of men. The blame rests with Saul and the wicked woman for practicing it.

God has a way of turning the evil actions and practices of men into something that he can use to further his cause, be it judgment or salvation. This is his sovereign plan, and the cross is a perfect illustration of that.

37

Sweat Like Drops of Blood

≡ LUKE 22:39–46 ≡

I believe humankind is incapable of grasping the sheer weight of what Jesus felt as he drew near to the cross. Jesus knew it was the Father's will that he would go to the cross. It was the only way our redemption could be accomplished. One perfect man would become the one perfect and atoning sacrifice for human sin.

Jesus told his disciples on numerous occasions about God's plan.

> "See, we are going up to Jerusalem. And the Son of Man will be delivered over to the chief priests and scribes, and they will condemn him to death and deliver him over to the Gentiles to be mocked and flogged and crucified, and he will be raised on the third day."
>
> Matthew 20:18–19

It seems clear to us on this side of the cross. But for the disciples, it was a little confusing because it clearly contradicted their view of

202

who the Messiah was to be and what he would do. In their minds, the Messiah would not die but would lead Israel out of political and militaristic oppression. He would even lead a spiritual revival that would restore the Jews to their homeland and to their God all at the same time. By watching his miracles, listening to his word, and recognizing his authority, they, with God's help, rightly believed in him and identified him as the prophesied Messiah.[1]

But they could not fully understand until later why Jesus had to die and be raised to life first. The penalty for sin had to be paid. God's wrath needed to be absorbed and quenched while the tyranny brought about by sin and death was to be defeated and disarmed.

The weight of this responsibility lay on Jesus' shoulders as he headed toward Jerusalem, knowing full well what would happen there. Toward the end of his earthly ministry and after his triumphal entry into Jerusalem on the colt of a donkey, Jesus declared,

> "The hour has come for the Son of Man to be glorified. Truly I tell you, unless a grain of wheat falls to the ground and dies, it remains by itself. But if it dies, it produces much fruit."
>
> John 12:23–24

Jesus knew that the spiritual harvest of fruit that would come as a result of his impending death and resurrection would make it all worth it. But the burden of that daunting task shook him to the core as a man, for soon after he said,

> "Now my soul is troubled. What should I say—Father, save me from this hour? But that is why I came to this hour. Father, glorify your name."
>
> John 12:27–28[2]

Imagine for a moment what Jesus was facing:

1. The One who had known nothing but perfect fellowship with the Father was going to experience a break in that fellowship while on the cross. (Matthew 27:46)

2. He was about to experience and carry all the spiritual guilt and shame of our sin as well as an agonizing and horrendous physical death. (Isaiah 53:4–6, 10; Galatians 3:13)

3. He was about to endure the wrath of God as the substitutionary sacrifice who would take our place and pay the punishment for sin. (2 Corinthians 5:21; Hebrews 7:27; 1 Peter 2:24–25)

Knowing he was about to bear the curse for our sin, Jesus felt the weight of it in his soul and was troubled. He poses a hypothetical question—"Should I ask to be spared from this?" He then answers it clearly. No—this is the reason why he came.

The prophet Isaiah had predicted this, and Jesus' soul was troubled for good reason. For the prophet's description of what was about to come surely registered in Jesus' mind. In their book *Pierced for Our Transgressions: Rediscovering the Glory of Penal Substitution*, Steve Jeffrey, Michael Ovey, and Andrew Sach share their astonishment as well as a gripping citation of Isaiah's prophecy concerning the death of Jesus, the Suffering Servant:

> From beginning to end, the passage emphasizes the appalling horror of what the Servant endured—far beyond what has ever been borne by any other human being.
>
> His appearance was so disfigured beyond that of any man
>   and his form marred beyond human likeness . . .
> He was despised and rejected by men,
>   a man of sorrows, and familiar with suffering.
> Like one from whom men hide their faces
>   he was despised . . .
> we considered him stricken by God,
>   smitten by him, and afflicted . . .
> But he was pierced . . .
>   he was crushed . . .
> He was oppressed and afflicted . . .
>   he was led like a lamb to the slaughter . . .

> By oppression and judgment he was taken away
> . . . he was cut off from the land of the living . . .
> he was stricken . . .
> he poured out his life unto death. (Isaiah 52:14; 53:3–5,
>   7–8, 12)

What more could Isaiah possibly have said to emphasize the unimaginable, unparalleled anguish the Servant endured?[3]

It is no wonder that when Jesus entered the garden of Gethsemane to pray on the night before he was to be arrested, brought to trial, beaten and flogged, and crucified, he was affected by the gravity of it all such that he was "deeply distressed and troubled."

It wasn't that he was afraid of death in a general sense, but it was the *kind* of death he would endure that shook him. He was about to face the wrath of God in all its fury because he was about to "become sin for us" (2 Corinthians 5:21). The sinless Christ would face God's wrath for our sin. This is why Jesus said, "I am deeply grieved to the point of death" (Mark 14:34) and prayed for the "cup of God's wrath" that was to be poured out on him on the cross to be taken from him.

Any normal human being would ask for that, but he knew this was not to happen, and in his willingness to die for us he said, "Nevertheless, not what I will, but what you will" (Mark 14:36). The gospel of Luke gives us even more information, telling us that as he prayed by himself in these moments, an angel from heaven came to strengthen him since the emotional, spiritual, and physical anguish was so great. One might imagine that any normal human being could have been a candidate for a heart attack in this situation.

Then Luke tells us something incredible that reveals the depth of pain in Jesus' soul.

> Being in anguish, he prayed more fervently, and his sweat became like drops of blood falling to the ground.
>
> Luke 22:44

The intensity of the situation caused Jesus to go even deeper in prayer, and the anguish caused him to literally sweat. Luke describes his perspiration in a metaphorical sense as if it were like blood falling to the ground.

In the same way that at Jesus' baptism the Spirit descended upon him *like* a dove, where no physical bird actually landed on him, here the phrase that is translated *"like* drops of blood" is another metaphorical description (technically, a simile) that should not be taken literally. Rather, it is a way to describe the emotional suffering Jesus was enduring.[4] Darrell Bock explains,

> It is important to note that this is metaphorical, not a description that says Jesus sweat blood. The remark depicts Jesus' emotional state as so intense that he perspired profusely as a result. The sweat beads multiplied on his body like flowing clumps of blood and dropped to the earth.[5]

Simile or no simile, the anguish was excruciating.[6] Interestingly, though the word *like* puts a crimp on us seeing him as having sweat actual blood, a medical condition known as *hematidrosis* can cause one's blood vessels to dilate and burst, causing sweat and blood to mix when under extreme strain. Could that have happened here? Anything is possible, but if it did happen, Luke probably would not have used the comparative word *like*.

Either way, this simile is powerful in that it paints a picture of a man who is exploding with sorrow and anguish. Indeed, Jesus' physical suffering began long before they beat, scourged, and crucified him. The use of metaphors and similes in the Bible helps us understand many things that are not otherwise understandable to us. But since it would be difficult for us to truly understand the stress Jesus was under, this simile of sweating "like drops of blood" helps us to imagine to a small degree what he might have felt.[7]

Incredible. He took the wrath of God so that whoever believes in him will not have to for all eternity. What wondrous love is this? Thank you, Jesus. Thank you.

38

A Footrace to the Tomb

≡ JOHN 20:1–10 ≡

Growing up, my favorite stories were from the original *Winnie the Pooh*, written in the 1920s by A. A. Milne. Along with Pooh, the fictional characters of Piglet, Eeyore, Kanga, Roo, and Tigger seemed to entertain and capture the imagination, and the young boy, Christopher Robin, was a character based on Milne's own son, Christopher Robin Milne.

The creativity, poetic language, humor, attention to details, and captivating story line has a way of grabbing our attention and pricking our imaginations. In Pooh's world, we experience the innocence of childhood coupled with lessons on life and friendship.

Many of us also love stories of good versus evil. Battles between heroes and villains feed our competitive spirits while drawing us into a world of imagination and fun. The recent *Marvel* movies are a perfect example. We love stories of victory, redemption, and the triumph of good over evil.

The common link to all of this is our imagination. It is a powerful tool; our imaginations are often stronger in our minds than in our eyes. In other words, many people say that when they see a movie based on a book they liked, they end up a little disappointed and may comment that they like the book better. Why is that? Because our minds create the images and feelings that sometimes movies cannot do.

In the same way, the Bible has stories that grip us, entertain us, and feed our imaginations. It too has unique characters along with moments of suspense, intense situations, humor, and surprise. And there is no greater story than the victory over death that the disciples and followers of Jesus witnessed on Resurrection Sunday some two thousand years ago. But unlike the fictional stories noted above, this story is true and complete with many riveting details.

The apostle John, in his gospel story, includes an unusual detail that will forever be part of the narrative of that special morning when Jesus was raised from the dead. I will quote John's account from John 20:1–10, and highlight what seems odd to mention in the midst of the story.

> Now on the first day of the week Mary Magdalene came to the tomb early, while it was still dark, and saw that the stone had been taken away from the tomb. So she ran and went to Simon Peter and the other disciple, the one whom Jesus loved, and said to them, "They have taken the Lord out of the tomb, and we do not know where they have laid him." So Peter went out with the other disciple, and they were going toward the tomb. *Both of them were running together, but the other disciple outran Peter and reached the tomb first.* And stooping to look in, he saw the linen cloths lying there, but he did not go in. Then Simon Peter came, following him, and went into the tomb. He saw the linen cloths lying there, and the face cloth, which had been on Jesus' head, not lying with the linen cloths but folded up in a place by itself. Then the other disciple, who had reached the tomb first, also went in, and he saw and believed; for as yet they did not understand the Scripture, that he must rise from the dead. Then the disciples went back to their homes.
>
> John 20:1–10 esv, emphasis mine

It might not seem significant compared to the overall story line here, but why does John say "the other disciple" outran Peter and reached the tomb first? Most scholars believe that all throughout the gospel of John, when John mentions "the disciple whom Jesus loved," he is likely referring to himself.[1] If true, John, for some reason, has forever included in history his foot speed in comparison to Peter's physical prowess.

But why? Was there a rivalry of some type between the two, and John wanted to take a quick brotherly jab at his buddy? Or is there something else going on here? The speculations and educated guesses abound. Some say John outran him simply because he had a greater love for Jesus. Doubtful. Others say John was a more eager follower of Christ with more faith, and therefore he ran harder than Peter. Unlikely.

Some go even further and assign symbolism and allegory to the whole thing. D. A. Carson gives us details:

> As for the allegorical interpretations that have attached themselves to theses verses, there is too little evidence to support any of them. There is no indication, for instance, that the description of the beloved disciple's fleetness of foot—swifter than Peter!—is a veiled way of insisting that in the "Johannine church" John must be accorded greater pre-eminence than Peter . . . even the suggestion is repulsive. Bultmann holds that Peter represents Jewish Christianity, and the beloved disciple represents Gentile Christianity: the Jewish church is first on the scene (Peter enters the tomb before John), but that fact gives no precedence since both stand beside the empty grave-clothes. Indeed the eager faith of the Gentiles is greater than the Jews (the beloved disciple ran faster than Peter). *There are no reliable indications in the text that John assigned such symbolic value to the two disciples.* The ancient explanation for the swiftness of the beloved disciple is probably the correct one: he was younger than Peter, and arrived first.[2]

In other words, what Carson clearly tells us is that it is unwise and even in some instances repulsive to start reading into the text certain ideas that simply are not there. Unfortunately, some Bible interpreters do this all the time. They neglect a literal reading of the text and opt for more of a symbolic or allegorical meaning at the expense of missing the simple truths of the story.

This kind of approach to interpreting Scripture must be avoided. Unless it is obvious that the Bible is using symbolic or figurative language, we must always interpret it literally and at face value. Otherwise, people can make the Bible say whatever they want to fit their agenda.

The fact is, John included these details because *it is exactly how it happened*, and it is unlikely that it is for any other reasons than that. Carson concludes, "Because the entire narrative is designed to explain just how and when and to what degree faith in the resurrection was achieved (cf. vv. 29–31), the details of the eyewitness are deemed important."[3]

These are the things that make for a good true story. Facts. Details. The little things that help our minds paint the scene for ourselves. John was a master at it, a good storyteller. In fact, I believe his gospel is the most engaging because he knew how to tell the story well.

The story John tells has all the ingredients for a good story, but not just any story—the most important story on earth. For the good news is that Jesus has indeed been raised from the dead, conquering sin, death, and the grave. It is a story of good triumphing over evil. It has characters, details, and a captivating storyline. But this is no fictional story. This story is real, and it can have a real and eternal impact on those who read it with the eyes of faith.

We cannot read into it what isn't there. Instead, what is there has to be read into us.

39

The Romantic Wording in Song of Songs

I don't need to tell you that today's culture is infatuated with sex. At almost every turn we are confronted with it. Something that God intended to be enjoyed and celebrated has been ripped from its proper context and has done irreparable harm throughout the history of humanity. Like fire in a fireplace, when it is kept where it should be—as part of a marriage covenant between a man and a woman—it can be beautiful. But if it leaves that fireplace and falls out of the proper context, it can burn and consume anything it touches, destroying relationships, families, and ultimately people.

The Bible is not afraid to tackle the subject of sex, which is why we need to look at the perplexing language of Song of Songs (or Song of Solomon). When we were kids, this is the book of the Bible our parents often worried about us reading, but that was never God's intent. It was designed to be a series of love poems used to describe the joys and blessings of sex between a husband and wife. In this sense, it is one of the more positive perspectives of sex that the Bible presents.

At the same time, we must admit that most of the narrative accounts in the Bible demonstrate how we have found a way to corrupt something God designed to be good and beautiful. Israel was constantly tempted by the pagan nations and their methods of worship that involved fertility cults and temple prostitution. Rape, incest, and abuse are all found in the Scriptures, revealing to us the depth of our depravity.

But God designed the marriage bed to be a different story, as the proper use of sex sees it both as a means of *procreation* as well as an *expression of covenant love* for the purposes of pleasure and intimacy. God wants married couples to enjoy all of what he intended for it to be. We ought not to forfeit his best for us by misusing it.

The fire in the fireplace illustration is a common metaphor used for sex. Metaphors have a way of connecting with us and speaking to us in ways we can understand. They are powerful tools, used often in poetry and songs to evoke emotion and stimulate the mind. The Song of Songs is no exception.

But throughout the history of the church, some people have radically misinterpreted this book of the Bible. One of the more common misuses was the allegorical approach, where the descriptive language of the song was interpreted in such a way that the words and thoughts stood for something other than what was literally said, usually something more *spiritual and hidden* in nature.

Some see the song as a metaphor for the history of the Israelites. Others see it as a story of love, either between God and Israel, or as a description of the love that Christ has for his church (i.e., the Bridegroom and the bride of Christ). But the most convincing method of interpretation is the literal meaning of the words as a description of married love. Tremper Longman explains,

> The literal/natural reading of the Song resists the idea that the Song is a code, saying something different than the words imply.

There is no need for a special key to unlock the code, but rather the interpreter applies the same principles to the Song as he or she would do to any other comparable writing. It is necessary, though, to point out immediately that literal does not mean a flat or plain interpretation. A natural reading affirms the presence of rich poetry with all the ambiguity and mystery inherent in that poetry.[1]

In other words, we should interpret the song literally unless it is obvious that figurative or metaphorical language is being used. So when it says "your breasts are like two fawns" (Song of Songs 2:5), we do not take it to mean that she has two literal animals on her body, but rather there is something about her breasts that remind the husband of something that is true about two fawns of the forest. And the more we know about fawns, the more we will understand what the author meant by this.

This is really the key to interpreting the song or poem that is the Song of Songs in the Bible. We interpret it as "an anthology of love poems, a kind of erotic psalter . . . [and] the pressing concern of exegesis of the Song is unpacking the metaphors and explaining the effect that it has on us as readers."[2] To understand it better, we must put ourselves into the mindset and culture of ancient Near Eastern culture, language, imagery, and typology. Let's take a quick look at some of the romantic poetry of Song of Songs (we will choose some selections from chapter 4), so that we can more clearly grasp its ideas.

> How beautiful you are, my darling. How very beautiful! Behind your veil, your eyes are doves. Your hair is like a flock of goats streaming down Mount Gilead.
>
> Song of Songs 4:1

Here we see the use of a metaphor and a simile. He begins with a *metaphor* when he says, "your eyes are doves." He is not talking literally here, but rather in a figurative sense; he is comparing her eyes to traits that are also recognizable about a dove. This means that we should do some background study on doves, which are beautiful creatures often prized for their soft feathers and the gentleness of their flight. Could it be that the lover is complimenting the softness and gentleness of his wife's eyes? This is likely the case.

As a reminder of what we just learned in chapter 37, similes are almost identical to metaphors in that we are comparing two similar things, but the simile merely adds a word by using the terms *as* or *like*. Solomon says that his bride's hair "is *like* a flock of goats streaming down Mount Gilead." I can't imagine any husband saying that to his wife today, but back in that day and in that context it meant something truly beautiful.

Again, this is where further digging is needed. Goats have not always been portrayed positively in Scripture. They were used in the Old Testament as a picture of sin and were used readily in the sacrificial system of Israel. And even in the New Testament, Jesus told the parable of the sheep and the goats, whereby the sheep are portrayed as believers who are blessed at the second coming and the goats represent unbelievers who are cursed and judged by God.

But there is another sense in which goats are seen more in a positive light in the Bible. Goat hair was the main ingredient in extremely valuable clothing; even cashmere today is made from goat hair.[3] Further, the curtains of the sacred tabernacle were made from the hair of goats. So the husband is likely not saying his wife's hair reminds him of sin or judgment, but rather he sees her flowing and streaming hair as a valuable asset to her beauty, reminding him of the softest and most valuable clothing, perhaps even something sacred.

This is the approach we must take when we interpret this kind of ancient poetry or love song. So when he says, "*Your teeth are like a flock of newly shorn sheep . . . your lips are like a scarlet cord . . . your neck is like the tower of David . . . and your breasts are like two fawns, twins of a gazelle that feed among the lilies,*" we know there is much beauty in what he is saying as he compares her body to some of the most desirable things on earth as he knows it. We simply need to do our homework and go on a treasure hunt in order to find out the value of these similes and metaphors.[4]

But leaving the metaphors behind, there are times when he will also come right out and say in the most straightforward fashion:

> You are absolutely beautiful, my darling; there is no imperfection in you.
>
> Song of Songs 4:7

I, for one, am so glad that poems and songs like this are in the Bible. They redeem an often taboo subject. Perhaps the words and insights of Old Testament scholar Tremper Longman offer the most helpful conclusion as to why this is in our Bibles. He writes,

> Without the Song, the Church and the synagogue would be left with spare and virtually exclusively negative words about an important aspect of our lives. Sexuality is a major aspect of the human experience, and God in his wisdom has spoken through the poet(s) of the Song to encourage as well as warn us about its power in our lives. God is interested in us as a whole people. We are not souls encased in a husk of flesh. The Song celebrates the joys of physical touch, the exhilaration of exotic scents, the sweet sound of an intimate voice, the taste of another's body. Furthermore the book explores human emotion—the thrill and power of love as well as its often attendant pain. The Song affirms human love, intimate relationship, sensuality, and sexuality.[5]

Since the world is consumed with sex in the wrong way, maybe it is time that we preach and teach about it in the right way. The Song of Songs helps us do that. God, in his infinite wisdom, knew this, and this is why he, through the inspired words of the Holy Spirit, made sure that it was to be found in our Bibles.

40

Child Sacrifice

≡ 2 Kings 16, 21 ≡

Ask any parent, and one of their most important priorities is to protect their children. In an age where mass shootings in schools have become all too common, a parent's biggest nightmare is encountering anything that could do any level of harm to their children, no matter what age they are. As the psalmist writes, "Behold, children are a heritage from the LORD, the fruit of the womb a reward" (Psalm 127:3 ESV).

Perhaps nothing is more detestable in all of the Bible than the ancient Canaanite practice of child sacrifice. The Ammonites and Moabites practiced it in sacrifice to their gods, Molech and Chemosh.[1] Whereas in Israel the firstborn son was especially worthy of double honor, in these pagan nations, the firstborn son (or daughter) was often the one worthy of sacrifice. Often it was done to appease these gods or to call on them in times of emergencies (cf. 2 Kings 3:26–27).

In Israel, the law of Moses was abundantly clear that this practice was never to be seen and was strictly forbidden, with the harshest of penalties if it was ever found among them.

> You are not to sacrifice any of your children in the fire to Molech. Do not profane the name of your God; I am the LORD.
>
> Leviticus 18:21

> The LORD spoke to Moses: "Say to the Israelites: Any Israelite or alien residing in Israel who gives any of his children to Molech must be put to death; the people of the country are to stone him. I will turn against that man and cut him off from his people, because he gave his offspring to Molech, defiling my sanctuary and profaning my holy name."
>
> Leviticus 20:1–3

Yet Israel fell hard into the idolatry of the surrounding peoples, even adopting this horrific practice throughout different periods of its history. One of the indictments that the LORD laid upon Israel and Judah for sending them both into exile was the fact that they practiced this.

> They have built the high places of Baal in Ben Hinnom Valley to sacrifice their sons and daughters in the fire to Molech—something I had not commanded them. I had never entertained the thought that they do this detestable act causing Judah to sin!
>
> Jeremiah 32:35

To God, this was an abomination, and it ought to feel that way to us as well. Nothing is more heinous than the purposeful murder of innocent children, be it inside or outside the womb. How hardened does one's heart have to be in order to allow their children to scream in pain as they pass through the fire of sacrifice? Yet this was what this practice mandated, and when offered up, the pagan priests would clap loudly or bang on drums in order to drown out the cries. This is satanic.

Of all the people who were charged with leading and protecting the Israelites, one would think the kings of Israel and Judah would have quickly squashed any form of this awful practice. But what we find in Scripture is the opposite. Not only did they fail to suppress it, but they practiced it themselves.

The first mention of an Israelite king tolerating the gods of these pagan peoples is found in 1 Kings 11, where David's son Solomon, whose heart had been turned away by his marriages to foreign women, did what was evil in the sight of the LORD by building places of worship for these deities.

> For when Solomon was old his wives turned away his heart after other gods, and his heart was not wholly true to the LORD his God, as was the heart of David his father. For Solomon went after Ashtoreth the goddess of the Sidonians, and after Milcom the abomination of the Ammonites. So Solomon did what was evil in the sight of the LORD and did not wholly follow the LORD, as David his father had done. Then Solomon built a high place for Chemosh the abomination of Moab, and for Molech the abomination of the Ammonites, on the mountain east of Jerusalem. And so he did for all his foreign wives, who made offerings and sacrificed to their gods.
>
> 1 Kings 11:4–8 ESV

Though the text does not say that Solomon himself offered his children in sacrifice, he was equally complicit and guilty of it, as he enabled his foreign wives to worship these deities by building altars to them. As a result, Solomon's kingdom was torn into the two kingdoms of Israel (north) and Judah (south). Further, the kings who followed him who also turned away from the LORD caused even more judgment to fall on the Israelites.

Two of those wicked kings that engage in the sacrifice of children were King Ahaz (731–715 BC) and King Manasseh (687–642 BC) of the Southern Kingdom of Judah. Ahaz was co-regent at times with his father (Jotham, who was actually a good king) and his son (Hezekiah, another good king), but his legacy was anything but good. He was twenty years old when he began his reign that would last sixteen years.

> He did not do what was right in the sight of the LORD his God like his ancestor David but walked in the ways of the kings of Israel. He even sacrificed his son in the fire, imitating the detestable practices of the nations the LORD had dispossessed before the Israelites. He sacrificed and burned incense on the high places, on the hills, and under every green tree.
>
> 2 Kings 16:2–4

This king in multiple ways profaned the name of the LORD and engaged in the detestable by offering up and sacrificing an Israelite prince to the pagan gods. This is the first biblical record of this kind of sacrifice being offered up by an Israelite, and thus Ahaz is credited with bringing in this practice.[2]

Though Ahaz was graciously followed by one of the best kings in the history of Judah (Hezekiah), Ahaz's grandson Manasseh (just twelve years old when he assumed his kingship) was just like his grandfather.

> He did what was evil in the LORD's sight, imitating the detestable practices of the nations that the LORD had dispossessed before the Israelites. He rebuilt the high places that his father Hezekiah had destroyed and reestablished the altars for Baal. He made an Asherah, as King Ahab of Israel had done; he also bowed in worship to all the stars in the sky and served them. He built altars in the LORD's temple, where the LORD had said, "Jerusalem is where I will put my name." He built altars to all the stars in the sky in both courtyards of the LORD's temple. He sacrificed his son in the fire, practiced witchcraft and divination, and consulted mediums and spiritists. He did a huge amount of evil in the LORD's sight, angering him.
>
> 2 Kings 21:2–6

King Manasseh reigned in Jerusalem for fifty-five years, and it was fifty-five years of paganism. He worshiped false gods, even the stars, and defiled the temple with pagan altars. But like his grand-father, he too "sacrificed his son in the fire" (v.6) and engaged in occult practices. One could say that Satan had a field day during this king's reign, such that Ahaz was said to do a "huge amount of evil in the LORD's sight" (v.6), shedding "so much innocent blood that he filled Jerusalem with it from one end to another" (2 Kings 21:16).

As a result of his wickedness, God pronounced judgment on the city of Jerusalem and the nation of Judah as a whole. It is said that Manasseh did more evil than the pagan peoples, the Amorites, who preceded him (2 Kings 21:11). No wonder the Babylonian exile was so harsh. The Judahites had stored up the wrath of God from all the evil done during this time.

What are we to make of these horrible realities? This is obvi-ously a historical and descriptive account of kings who did not love or regard the God of Israel in any way. They represent some of the darkest times of the Old Testament (except for maybe the period of the judges). The sacrificing of children is a demonically inspired worship practice that is essentially destroying someone made in God's image, and being that it is children, it is also the most vulnerable and precious of God's creation.

More than that, it was also designed by Satan to profane and mock God and his people, using no less than the kings of Israelite blood to do it. One could hear Satan's mockery: "See how far 'God's people' have come?" They could not even rightly be called God's people [by faith], which is why they fell into his wrath. Thankfully, God always preserved a remnant of godly Israelites.

In history, the Aztecs, Incas, and Mayans all practiced child sacrifice. The ancient Phoenicians and pagan Arabians did it as well. Even today, some witch doctors in Africa (especially Uganda) still practice child sacrifice as offerings.

We must remember that Satan is all about enslaving human beings into a life of sin and death. These terrible practices warn us and remind us how important it is to protect our children from the grips of evil, for Satan is constantly waging war against the most helpless and vulnerable. One of the many ways we protect our children is by raising them in the "fear and admonition" of the LORD, providing them a home that is filled with love for Christ and his Word. If only Israel and Judah would have clung to God's Word, things might have been different.

By example and by training, we can help spare our children the grief that comes from a fallen world that desires to devour them. Through Moses, God told the Israelites that they were to teach the Word of God to their children:

> These words that I am giving you today are to be in your heart. Repeat them to your children. Talk about them when you sit in your house and when you walk along the road, when you lie down and when you get up. Bind them as a sign on your hand and let them be a symbol on your forehead. Write them on the doorposts of your house and on your city gates.
>
> Deuteronomy 6:6–9

The stories we have just read reveal the very depths of human depravity. In my opinion, the modern-day abortion industry is equally as grotesque as the ancient offerings to Molech. This time the screams are silent but no less prevalent. I pray that in my lifetime I will see the end of this barbaric practice in the United States and elsewhere.

The gospel of Jesus Christ is the only hope for a world where this exists. For the one true God who walked this earth first appeared not as a grown man, but as a baby, a son, a firstborn son. And in order to redeem us from the bondage to sin and death, he offered himself up *not to Satan, but to God*, as a *willing* sacrifice for sin. Therein lies the difference. There is only one God whose wrath needed to be appeased, and Jesus Christ has done it on our behalf. The holiness of God was offended, and our Savior took it upon himself to absorb the wrath due to sin so that we might be saved from it.

Let us teach these truths to our children, whose lives are precious gifts to us from God. Let us seek to protect them from evil, teach them the truths of God's Word, and pray that they will come to know the God who loves them and died for them and, even better, is risen from the dead.

For there is nothing more beautiful than seeing our children become "oaks of righteousness" (Isaiah 61:3) so that they in turn can willingly offer up their lives in worship and service to the true King of Israel, the one who "gave *himself* for our sins to deliver us from the present evil age" (Galatians 1:4 ESV).

Conclusion

A hard part of writing a book like this is deciding what to cover and what to leave out. Many more stories and verses are worthy of note. As mentioned earlier, the entire book of Judges is a candidate because practically every story captures some of the most bizarre and darkest moments in Israelite history. We did not even cover the "death by tent peg" in Judges 4, the "foolish vow" of a father that led to the sacrifice of his own daughter in Judges 11, or the secret word of Judges 12 that could get you exposed and killed if you did not say it right.

Other stories and ideas surrounding the Bible have been debated by scholars and believers alike for centuries, like the age of the earth (Genesis 1), the question of guardian angels (Acts 12), and whether Christ did or did not descend into hell as the Apostles' Creed seemingly suggests. These topics have been written about elsewhere, and it is a healthy exercise to research, study, and compare scholarly research so as to come to some conclusions.

Through this book, I pray you have discovered interesting and enlightening truths that will whet your appetite for even more that the Bible offers. We live in a world and in a country where biblical illiteracy is widespread and growing, even in the church. It is time once again for Christians to be known as people of the

Book. We will never know our God the way he intended for us to know him unless we return to diligent study, sound exegetical and theologically rich preaching, memorization, and Word-centered discipleship.[1] We cannot relegate the study of God's Word only to Bible colleges and seminaries. It must begin and thrive in the home and in the local church.

When the Bible is properly understood in its own context, it must be believed, applied, and lived out faithfully by those who seek to be obedient to its truths. There is always blessing that comes when we obey God's moral laws and commands. His intent is for us to know him and glorify him and to spread his gospel to the ends of the earth. The Bible changes hearts, changes minds, and changes lives. It is God's agent for spiritual transformation and the message of hope for eternal life.

More than anything, the Bible is a story about God, centered on the person and work of Jesus Christ, to whom all Scripture testifies. We enter into a relationship with this God through repentance and faith as described by the testimonies, stories, and teachings of God's Word (the story of the gospel, which is the "good news" about Jesus' life, death, and resurrection from the dead).

My prayer is that you will hunger for the deep truths of God even more after reading this book, not just for its entertainment value, but for its saving and life-transforming power. This is the real truth about God and the real truth about us. The fact that the Bible is sacred will be true for all eternity. For "the grass withers, the flowers fade, but the word of our God remains forever" (Isaiah 40:8).

Notes

Chapter 1 Abraham and Isaac: The Sacrifice

1. The LORD required Abraham and his family to undergo circumcision, which would be a sign and distinctive symbol of all who were from Abraham's lineage. The cutting of the foreskin helped prevent the spread of disease and therefore had many health benefits, but ultimately it symbolized the need to be cut off from sin in a spiritual sense. Thus, the need to be cleansed from sin was what physical circumcision was meant to communicate. Paul would later tell us that the ultimate circumcision was the circumcision of our spiritual hearts, a heart that is cleansed by God's grace through belief in the gospel of Jesus Christ (Romans 2:29).

2. Before this, Sarah convinced Abraham to practice the custom of the day, which was to have relations with her Egyptian handmaid in order to produce a son Sarah could adopt as her own. This attempt to take matters into their own hands did in fact produce a son, named Ishmael, but he was not the promised child.

3. Yet the LORD made sure that they were to be taken care of (see Genesis 21:9–20).

Chapter 2 Hate Your Family?

1. Sarah Eekhoff Zylstra, "The Top 50 Countries Where It's Most Dangerous to Follow Jesus," *Christianity Today*, January 10, 2018, www.christianitytoday.com/news/2018/january/top-50-christian-persecution-open-doors-world-watch-list.html.

2. Darrell L. Bock, *Baker Exegetical Commentary on the New Testament: Luke 9:51–24:53* (Grand Rapids, MI: Baker Books, 1996), 1284.

3. Bock, *Baker Exegetical Commentary on the New Testament*, 1285.

4. John MacArthur, *The MacArthur New Testament Commentary: Luke 11–17* (Chicago: Moody Publishers, 2013), 283–284, second emphasis mine.

5. MacArthur, *The MacArthur New Testament Commentary: Luke 11–17*, 283–284.

Chapter 3 An Annoyed Apostle Takes Action

1. Darrell Bock, *Acts: Baker Exegetical Commentary on the New Testament* (Grand Rapids, MI: Baker Academic, 2007), 536, emphasis mine.

2. I believe the ability to cast out demons is a supernatural power that Christ uniquely gave to his apostles in order to authenticate their authority as spokesmen for God (connected even to their authority to later write what we know today as Scripture)—see Mark 3:15; 2 Corinthians 12:12.

Chapter 4 Balaam and the Talking Donkey

1. This becomes evident in Numbers 25 when apparently upon Balaam's advice (Numbers 31:16), the people of Israel fall into sexual sin with the Moabite and Midianite women who eventually help lead them into worship of their pagan fertility god, Baal of Peor (Numbers 25:3). The fact that Balaam (a pagan) hears the LORD is a precursor to the phenomenon that the donkey will hear and see the LORD as well, something we would not expect to happen.

2. Some suggest the angel of the LORD is a temporary manifestation of God himself here as he is in other contexts (e.g., Genesis 16:7; Exodus 3:2), but it is possible that this angel is to be distinguished from the LORD himself, since later in verse 31, Balaam's eyes are opened by the LORD in order to see the angel of the LORD. Either way, the angel will only speak what God himself wants to be said (compare vv. 20 and 35), as Timothy R. Ashley has pointed out in his commentary. Timothy R. Ashley, *The New International Commentary on the Old Testament: Numbers* (Grand Rapids, MI: Eerdmans Publishing, 1993), 455.

3. The Hebrew word for *donkey* is in the feminine form, and thus I am referring to it as a "she." Normally, male donkeys were used for riding, and there is a different masculine form of the word *donkey*, but that form is not found here. Therefore, we are dealing with a female donkey, as verse 28 confirms.

4. I am compelled to think that nature has more trust in its creator than sinful, unbelieving man does, if we are allowed to personify nature as Paul did in Romans 8:22.

5. Ashley, *Numbers*, 457.

Chapter 5 "Emasculate Themselves!"

1. This is not to suggest that Paul was perfect or sinless; rather, it means that he was in good standing in relationship to the law, externally conforming to it and always employing the proper means to stay in good relationship with it (the proper sacrifices and offerings) if there was ever a temporary breach.

2. Saul was his Hebrew name and Paul was his Greek name. Contrary to what many have thought, he did not go through a name change at his conversion but was rather addressed as Paul once he was commissioned to bring the gospel to the Gentiles, who were primarily Greek (see Acts 13:9).

3. Another driving force behind some of the false teachers may have been a racially charged hatred for some of the Gentiles, and by requiring them to follow Jewish customs (which most had never done before and would likely never do), they hoped to naturally alienate those who didn't look or act like upstanding Jews

(which is what the false teachers hoped to be seen as). Either way, we know the false teachers wanted to be seen as popular (Galatians 4:17) and impressive (Galatians 6:12), even though they were actually wimps wanting to avoid the persecution from unbelieving Jews that the Christ followers were receiving (Galatians 6:12).

4. Philip Graham Ryken, *Galatians: Reformed Expository Commentary* (Phillipsburg, NJ: P & R Publishing, 2005), 210.

Chapter 6 Justification by Faith Alone?

1. It is my contention that conversion includes the concepts of both repentance and faith, as Paul explains in Acts 26:20 when he said his message to the Gentiles was that they should "repent and turn to God [in faith]."

2. The Westminster Confession (1.9) tells us that "the infallible rule of interpretation of Scripture is the Scripture itself: and therefore, when there is a question about the true and full sense of any Scripture (which is not manifold, but one), it must be searched and known by other places that speak more clearly." As found at Theopedia, "Analogy of Faith," www.theopedia.com/analogy-of-faith.

Chapter 7 "Lead Us Not into Temptation"

1. Or "Evil One," as some manuscripts read.

2. Leah MarieAnn Klett, "Pope Francis approves change to the Lord's Prayer despite opposition: 'It's deeply problematic,'" *The Christian Post*, June 5, 2019, www.christianpost.com/news/pope-francis-approves-change-to-the-lords-prayer -despite-opposition-its-deeply-problematic.html.

3. D. A. Carson, *The Expositor's Bible Commentary: Matthew 1–12* (Grand Rapids, MI: Zondervan, 1995), 173.

4. John Piper, "Reading the Bible Upside Down," June 12, 2019, www.desiring god.org/articles/reading-the-bible-upside-down.

Chapter 8 Foreskins and Foolishness

1. A similar situation occurs later in the New Testament when Paul instructed that the sexually immoral man in Corinth was to be "handed over to Satan for the destruction of the flesh" (1 Corinthians 5:5). In these situations, God is simply withdrawing his hand of protection so that the afflicted person might repent and come back to God.

2. Perhaps David thought the sword would evoke fear in the Philistines and they would do whatever David asked of them, but we are not told exactly what David was thinking when he arrived.

3. John MacArthur, *The MacArthur Study Bible: NASB Updated Edition* (Nashville: Thomas Nelson, 2006), 404, note 21:13.

Chapter 9 The Finger on the Wall

1. The Phrase Finder, www.phrases.org.uk/meanings/count-your-chickens.html.

2. The Phrase Finder, www.phrases.org.uk/meanings/dont-throw-the-baby -out-with-the-bathwater.html. It has been speculated—likely improperly so—that

when a family took their weekly bath, the baby was the last one to be bathed and thus the water was rather murky by the time the bathing was done. When it was time to throw the used water out, one had to make sure the baby wasn't tossed out with it since it was so hard to see what was in there. I have my doubts as to whether the proverb had that as its background.

3. For more everyday phrases we often use that come from the Bible, see Paul Anthony Jones's article "18 Everyday Expressions Borrowed from the Bible," March 3, 2015, http://mentalfloss.com/article/61964/18-everyday-expressions-borrowed-bible.

4. For an excellent article on the progression of Nebuchadnezzar's saving faith as he encountered Daniel and others, see the ministry journal of Dr. Linus and Sharon Morris at One Expedition, February 7, 2011, https://onexpedition.org/2011/02/07/the-top-10-lessons-from-job/.

5. Leon Wood estimates that Daniel "had become an old man of about eighty-one years" about this time, having lived through the entire seventy years of exile that God's people had experienced in Babylon. See Leon Wood, *A Commentary on Daniel* (Eugene, OR: Wipf and Stock, 1998), 131. Wood's book was previously published by Zondervan in 1973.

6. These events are covered at the end of Daniel 4 in verses 28–37.

7. Scholarship is mixed on whether "Darius the Mede" was another name or honorable title for King Cyrus of Persia, who ended up ruling over this region, or whether Darius was Cyrus's general.

Chapter 10 Jesus and an Unfortunate Fig Tree

1. The Gospels record at least one other occasion (John 2:14–16) at the beginning of his ministry, along with what we have here in Mark (and in Matthew 21:12–13) of another cleansing toward the end of his ministry.

Chapter 11 A Message from God

1. Daniel Block notes that the cry of the Israelites is "not a cry of repentance or a plea for forgiveness; it is simply a cry of pain, a plea for divine aid." Daniel Block, *The New American Commentary: Judges, Ruth* (Nashville: Broadman and Holman, 1999), 159.

2. It is important to remember that not all the judges that God raised up were ideal role models (e.g., Samson), but nevertheless they accomplished the mission for the nation even if their own practices were not always ethically or morally acceptable. God uses imperfect people to carry out his will without necessarily endorsing the individual behavior of each deliverer.

3. Block, *New American Commentary: Judges, Ruth*, 162.

Chapter 12 An Ear Is Cut Off

1. To be fair, the foot-washing also set an example of what it meant to be a "servant leader," since the role of foot-washer was normally relegated to the common house servant whenever visitors would come in off the dusty roads of Palestine.

Chapter 13 Jeremiah's Linen Underwear

1. See Charles Feinberg, *Jeremiah: A Commentary* (Grand Rapids, MI: Zondervan, 1982) 106.

Chapter 14 The Nephilim: Who Were They?

1. Though the same word is translated (actually transliterated) as "Nephilim" after the flood in Numbers 13:33, when the Hebrew spies report back to Moses about the inhabitants of Canaan, this does not mean that this group of people was actually there in the land. If you read the passage carefully, you will see that the spies are prone to exaggeration, saying "they are stronger than we are" and "it is a land that devours its inhabitants" (Numbers 13:31–32 ESV). The spies further say that they saw the Nephilim, but the text clarifies that it is the sons of Anak who are being referred to—who come *from* the Nephilim—who were allegedly a group of very large, tall men who made the Israelite spies feel like "grasshoppers" in comparison. If it was truly the Nephilim that the spies saw, then this means they would have somehow survived the flood, which contradicts the idea that only Noah and his household survived (Genesis 6:17; 7:1). Further, the list of different peoples who inhabited the land from the book of Deuteronomy nowhere lists the Nephilim, and so as OT scholar Kenneth A. Mathews rightly suggests, "When we consider the evidence of Deuteronomy's recollection of these Canaanite peoples, it is better to understand the allusion to the Nephilim therefore in Numbers 13 as figurative, cited by the spies because of the violent reputation attributed to 'Nephilim' from ancient times." Kenneth A. Mathews, *The New American Commentary: Genesis 1–11:26* (Nashville: Broadman and Holman, 1996), 337.

2. Gleason Archer Jr., *New International Encyclopedia of Bible Difficulties* (Grand Rapids, MI: Zondervan, 1982), 79.

3. Archer, *New International Encyclopedia of Bible Difficulties*, 80.

4. Archer suggests, "What Genesis 6:1–2, 4 records is the first occurrence of mixed marriage between believers and unbelievers, with the characteristic result of such unions: complete loss of testimony for the LORD and a total surrender of moral standards," 80.

5. Mathews asserts that it was Julius Africanus (ca. AD 160–240) who was one of the first to suggest that the "sons of God" were descendants of Seth. Mathews, *The New American Commentary*, 329, footnote 105.

6. The *ESV Study Bible* (Wheaton, IL: Crossway Books, 2008), 61, footnote 6:1–2. For more study of the various views and theories and their strengths and weakness, there are some good online sites that give some quick summaries. See especially the article by Edward Antonio at Christianity.com, "Who Were the Nephilim in the Bible?" www.christianity.com/wiki/angels-and-demons/who-were-the-nephilim-in-the-bible.html. Another helpful overview comes from Bodie Hodge, "Nephilim, Who Were They?" Answers in Genesis, https://answersingenesis.org/bible-characters/who-were-the-nephilim/.

Chapter 15 "No One Knows the Day or the Hour"

1. A perfect example of how troubles, tests, and attacks are used by God to grow us up into mature character and thinking. The attacks of the "heretics" caused the

church to be strong in the knowledge of the Lord and his Word such that they needed to clearly and succinctly articulate the essential doctrines of the Christian faith.

2. This would certainly be true for Jesus prior to his resurrected and glorified state, the latter of which he now possesses.

3. Wayne Grudem, *Systematic Theology: An Introduction the Biblical Doctrine* (Grand Rapids, MI: Zondervan, 1994), 561. In addition, Jacques Dupuis asserts, "That the two natures do not mingle together by the hypostatic union—the human nature keeping its integrity—implies that the perfections of the divine nature, in this instance the divine knowledge, is not directly communicated to the human nature. That the two natures are not separated means that the human knowledge of Jesus is that of the Son of God." Jacques Dupuis, *Who Do You Say I Am? Introduction to Christology* (Maryknoll: Orbis Books, 1994), 119. In other words, *the entire* divine mind has not been communicated directly to Jesus' *human mind*, but what human knowledge he does have is that of the Word. This is a difficult concept to comprehend, for it would seem that if Jesus had two minds, then it would be most certain that the human mind would be completely aware of what is going on in the divine mind. But evidently this was not the case in Jesus as the previous Scriptures in Matthew and Mark show.

Chapter 16 A Nose Full of Quail

1. One can see here that Moses was carrying the burden of the Israelites and all their issues on a very personal level. Instead of going to the LORD, they go to him.

2. Many a pastor has probably said something similar in difficult moments of ministry, but God is always faithful, like he will be here for Moses.

3. As suggested by Timothy R. Ashley in *The Book of Numbers: New International Commentary on the Old Testament* (Grand Rapids, MI: Eerdmans Publishing, 1993), 219.

Chapter 17 Solomon's Many Wives

1. Though the subject of divorce is not our current focus, in my opinion, the only way in which the marriage bond is broken in a biblical sense is through death (1 Corinthians 7:39), the desertion and abandonment of an unbelieving spouse (1 Corinthians 7:15), or by adultery where reconciliation is not possible (Matthew 19:9).

2. Someone with this kind of sin demonstrates a narcissistic and addictive personality. But one must also simply leave room for the idea that he had simply been taken captive to all his fleshly desires without any limits.

3. Paul R. House, *The New American Commentary: 1, 2 Kings* (Nashville: Broadman and Holman, 1995), 174.

Chapter 18 Destroying the Soul and Body in Hell

1. A helpful discussion of the sense in which God can be in hell is found in Wayne Grudem's *Systematic Theology: An Introduction to Biblical Doctrine* (Grand Rapids, MI: Zondervan, 1994), 175–177.

2. Note that I am assuming the overwhelming biblical testimony of hell as a literal, physical place of torment for the wicked. The debate concerning its existence is not the present concern of this chapter.

3. Grudem uses Amos 9:1–4 as an example of the wicked's inability to escape God's presence in judgment (Grudem, *Systematic Theology*, 175).

4. Grudem, *Systematic Theology*, 175.

5. Grudem, *Systematic Theology*, 176.

Chapter 19 Herod Eaten by Worms

1. Merrill F. Unger, *The New Unger's Bible Dictionary* (Chicago: Moody Publishers, 1988), 602.

2. According to commentator Darrell Bock, the "occasion may be the quinquennial games at Caesarea, held in March, or Claudius' birthday in August if it is not a special convocation." Darrell L. Bock, *Acts: Baker Exegetical Commentary on the New Testament* (Grand Rapids, MI: Baker Academic, 2007), 431.

3. Josephus is even more specific, whereas Luke is likely a summary. Josephus states the people said, "Be thou merciful to us; for although we have hitherto reverenced thee only as a man, yet shall we henceforth own thee as superior to mortal nature." Josephus, *Antiquities of the Jews*, 19.8.2, 343, www.perseus.tufts .edu/hopper/text?doc=Perseus%3Atext%3A1999.01.0146%3Abook%3D19%3 Awhiston+chapter%3D8%3Awhiston+section%3D2.

4. Bock, *Acts: Baker Exegetical Commentary on the New Testament*, 431.

5. Ibid., 432.

Chapter 20 Send the Choir into Battle First

1. The Hebrew says Jehoshaphat "set his face to seek Yahweh, or to seek the Lord."

Chapter 21 Death at Communion

1. Even the apostle Paul was honest and open about his own personal struggle with sin in Romans 7.

2. For more on the nature and purpose of this divine discipline, see my book entitled *Love that Rescues: God's Fatherly Love in the Practice of Church Discipline* (Eugene, OR: Wipf and Stock Publishers, 2010), 176–181.

Chapter 22 A Youth Group Is Killed by Bears

1. Ahaziah's death is also attributed to his attempt to consult the false god Baal instead of the God of Israel as to whether or not he would recover from his fall. Elijah prophesied that due to Ahaziah's disobedient pursuit of Baal, he would never recover from his injuries (2 Kings 1:16).

2. They were mocking and jeering Elisha, much like the captains and their fifty men who came to make demands on Elijah but who experienced fire from heaven earlier in 2 Kings 1.

3. Paul R. House, *The New American Commentary: 1, 2 Kings* (Nashville: Broadman and Holman, 1995), 261.

Chapter 23 Not Peace but Division

1. F. F. Bruce, *The Hard Sayings of Jesus* (Downers Grove, IL: IVP Press, 1983), 131.

Chapter 24 Absalom's Head Stuck in a Tree

1. For another psalm of penitence by David that was likely written after Psalm 51, see Psalm 32.

Chapter 25 The Sun and Moon Stand Still

1. The book of Jashar was apparently an ancient collection of Israelite poems and songs that were used to remember the celebrations and victories of God's people and their leaders. Though no copies of the book seemingly exist today, the book is quoted here and also referred to in 2 Samuel 1:18.

2. John F. Walvoord and Roy B. Zuck, *The Bible Knowledge Commentary: Old Testament* (Colorado Springs: Cook Communications Ministries, 2004), 351.

Chapter 26 "Neither Jew nor Gentile . . . Male nor Female"

1. Al Mohler, "The Briefing" January 9, 2019, https://albertmohler.com/2019/01/09/briefing-1-9-19.

2. Anthony A. Hoekema, *Created in God's Image* (Grand Rapids, MI. Eerdmans Publishing, 1986), 150.

3. Andrew Walker, "The Christian Response to Gender Dysphoria," September 9, 2016, www.thegospelcoalition.org/article/the-christian-response-to-gender-dysphoria/.

4. We are equal in essence with different distinctions and roles (just like what we find within the triune Godhead).

Chapter 27 Ananias and Sapphira

1. One thing that is true in the Bible is that there are times when God's judgment is delayed. Perhaps it will happen later in life, it will await one's death, or it will even be revealed at the end of time at the great white throne judgment (Revelation 20:11–15). Or his judgment may happen instantaneously, as it did in one sense here.

Chapter 28 Handling Snakes and Drinking Poison

1. Within the historical evidence, there are two different endings to the gospel of Mark: a "shorter ending" and a "longer ending." Only the longer ending is usually included in our Bibles since there are more manuscripts that contain it than the shorter ending. (Only four manuscripts have the shorter ending, and they

date to the seventh to ninth centuries, making them less reliable.) But even in the manuscripts that include the longer ending, many scribal marks and asterisks indicate that the copyists thought that the longer ending was questionable at best.

2. James R. Edwards, *The Gospel According to Mark: The Pillar New Testament Commentary*, D. A. Carson, gen. ed. (Grand Rapids, MI: Eerdmans Publishing, 2002), 498–499.

3. For a helpful summary of the verses in Mark 16:9–20 that are corroborated elsewhere throughout the other gospel accounts and books of the New Testament, see John MacArthur, *The MacArthur New Testament Commentary, Mark 9–16* (Chicago: Moody Publishers, 2015), 413–415.

4. Paul told the Corinthians, "The signs of an apostle were performed with unfailing endurance among you, including signs and wonders and miracles" (2 Corinthians 12:12).

5. "2 Drink Strychnine at Service and Die in Display of Faith," *New York Times*, April 10, 1973, www.nytimes.com/1973/04/10/archives/2-drink-strychnine-at-service-and-die-in-display-of-faith.html.

6. Spencer Wilking and Lauren Effron, "Snake-Handling Pentecostal Pastor Dies From Snake Bite," ABC News, February 17, 2014, https://abcnews.go.com/US/snake-handling-pentecostal-pastor-dies-snake-bite/story?id=22551754.

7. Wilking and Effron, "Snake-Handling Pentecostal Pastor Dies From Snake Bite."

8. Julia Duin, "Death of snake handling preacher shines light on lethal Appalachian tradition," CNN, June 1, 2012, http://religion.blogs.cnn.com/2012/06/01/death-of-snake-handling-preacher-shines-light-on-lethal-appalachian-tradition/.

9. For more on the misuse of this Bible story as a means of discerning the will of God, see my book entitled *The Most Misused Stories in the Bible: Surprising Ways Popular Bible Stories are Misunderstood* (Minneapolis: Bethany House Publishers, 2017), 22–29.

10. The idea of "foxhole promises" comes from the idea that during a time of war, when someone is under fire from the enemy and feels pinned down in a pre-dug hole used for safety called a foxhole, they will make promises to God that are out of the ordinary if somehow they might be spared injury or death.

11. This is a rather large debate among scholars as to whether Mark ends at 16:8 too abruptly. Could it be the original ending was lost and has never been found, or did Mark intentionally end it this way in a fashion similar to his abrupt beginning where he immediately skips any birth narratives and goes right to the ministry of Jesus?

12. Robert H. Stein, *Mark: Baker Exegetical Commentary on the New Testament* (Grand Rapids, MI: Baker Academic, 2008), 727–728.

Chapter 29 The Battle for Moses' Body

1. Christopher Wright, *New International Biblical Commentary: Deuteronomy* (Peabody, MA: Hendrickson Publishers, 1996), 313.

2. One thing we cannot do is skip the point as to why Jude shared this insight into the heavenly realms with us. Though it helps us understand what happened

to Moses' body, his main point is to describe the ways that false teachers slander celestial beings and to show how inappropriate that is for us today since not even the archangel Michael slandered God back in the Old Testament. The false teachers were taking up authority that they had never been given and were committing blasphemy (Jude 10). Further, we should note that this story of Moses' body is also mentioned in the apocryphal book entitled *The Assumption of Moses*, a noncanonical book that may have informed Jude's writing without Jude actually endorsing the book.

Chapter 31 Bodily Discharges

1. Though they are experiencing a partial hardening during the church age (Romans 11:25), I believe that as a people group they are still a part of God's future plans as many will come to faith in their Messiah during the tribulation period (Zechariah 12:10; Revelation 7:1–8) and will be saved (Romans 11:26). God will one day restore Israel as a believing nation.

2. Within the tabernacle resided the ark of the covenant and other items used in Israelite worship.

3. John Hartley phrases it this way: "'Holiness' thus refers to Yahweh's inner nature and 'glory' to his outward appearing." John E. Hartley, *Leviticus: Word Biblical Commentary* (Dallas: Word Publishing, 1992), lvi.

4. Gordon Wenham remarks, "These laws have fascinated and perplexed generations of biblical scholars. Why did God decree that certain foods could be eaten and others must be rejected? There has been a great variety of suggestions but to this day no consensus has emerged." Gordon Wenham, *Leviticus: The New International Commentary on the Old Testament* (Grand Rapids, MI: Eerdmans Publishing, 1979), 165.

5. Hartley, *Leviticus*, lix.

6. "You must keep the Israelites from their uncleanness, so that they do not die by defiling my tabernacle that is among them" (Leviticus 15:31).

7. Wenham, *Leviticus*, 223.

8. Wenham, *Leviticus*, 223.

9. Wenham, *Leviticus*, 224.

Chapter 32 Resurrections at Christ's Death

1. Taken directly from James Montgomery Boice, *The Gospel of Matthew, Volume 2: An Expositional Commentary* (Grand Rapids, MI: Baker Books, 2001), 622.

2. Boice expands further and says that the tearing of the curtain taught three things: 1) "The old system of offering sacrifices year by year was over; 2) Jesus' offering of himself was the perfect and final sacrifice; so nothing more needs to be done to reconcile sinful men and women to God; 3) Because of Christ's work it is now possible for those who believe on him to approach God directly." Boice, *The Gospel of Matthew, Volume 2*, 624–625.

3. This is Boice's assertion.

4. Several theological reflections on these factual events are nicely covered by D. A. Carson in his commentary on the Gospel of Matthew, *The Expositor's Bible*

Commentary, Matthew Chapters 13 through 28 (Grand Rapids, MI: Zondervan, 1995), 582.

Chapter 33 Dismemberment of a Concubine

1. In the Old Testament it was permissible for priests to marry (see Leviticus 21:13–14), but sleeping with a concubine for sexual release or gratification was strictly forbidden since it was outside the bounds of marriage and considered "harlotry" (Leviticus 21:7).

2. Daniel Block, *The New American Commentary: Judges, Ruth* (Nashville: Broadman and Holman, 1999), 542.

3. Paul, in 1 Corinthians, tells us that the failures of Israel in the Old Testament wilderness experiences serve as "examples for us, that we might not desire evil as they did" (10:6 ESV).

Chapter 34 Head Coverings

1. The Greek words for *man* and *woman* can also be translated equally as *husband* and *wife* respectively, and since the issue is dealing with authority and submission in the context of important relationships, I have used the ESV's translation that appropriately sees the proper context for such authority and submission in the marriage relationships.

2. Many scholars argue that the idea of the "head" is to be understood as the "source" of the relationship, as in the "head of the river is its source." Others maintain that the word in the Greek is to be understood in reference to "authority." It is beyond the scope of this book to enter into that long and hotly debated discussion, but Wayne Grudem's analysis in his book *Evangelical Feminism: A New Path to Liberalism?* (Wheaton, IL: Crossway Publishers, 2006) has persuaded me that the better understanding is that the word is dealing with authority structures within relationships.

3. I realize this brings up a whole host of other topics and issues that are beyond the scope of this book, but I am under the conviction that the Scriptures teach that a godly man who loves his wife sacrificially and loves her as "Christ loved the church" (Ephesians 5:25) in order for her to grow spiritually (Ephesians 5:26–27) is charged with the primary role of spiritual leader in the marriage relationship.

4. John MacArthur, *The MacArthur New Testament Commentary: 1 Corinthians* (Chicago: Moody Press, 1984), 254.

5. *ESV Study Bible* (Wheaton, IL: Crossway, 2008), 2207, footnote 11:14.

Chapter 35 "Eat My Flesh and Drink My Blood"

1. For more on the type of accusations leveled against Christians, see Dr. Ken Curtis's (founding publisher of *Christian History* magazine) excellent summary in his article "Accusations," Christianity.com, April 28, 2010, www.christianity .com/church/church-history/timeline/1-300/accusations-11629581.html.

2. D. A. Carson remarks, "Any dullard could see that Jesus is not speaking literally: no-one would suppose Jesus was seriously advocating cannibalism and

offering himself as the first meal." D. A. Carson, *The Gospel According to John: The Pillar New Testament Commentary* (Grand Rapids, MI: Eerdmans Publishing, 1991), 295.

Chapter 36 Saul, a Medium-Spiritist, and the Spirit of Samuel

1. Bill T. Arnold, *The New Application Commentary: 1&2 Samuel* (Grand Rapids, MI: Zondervan, 2003), 375. I had the great privilege of studying Hebrew in seminary under Dr. Arnold, and his scholarship is impeccable.
2. The fact that Samuel says you will "be with me" is somewhat vague and puzzling. Is he referring to the "realm of the dead," the world beyond the grave? Is he talking about them being with him in the "abode of the righteous," or heaven itself? The latter would assume that Saul had a saving relationship with the Lord even in spite of his disobedience, which is possible. The answer is, we simply do not know the specifics of Samuel's referent here.
3. Arnold, *The New Application Commentary*, 378–379.

Chapter 37 Sweat Like Drops of Blood

1. Their ability to do this was assisted by God himself. For as Jesus said to Peter (who identified Jesus as the Christ): "Blessed are you, Simon son of Jonah, because flesh and blood did not reveal this to you, but my Father in heaven" (Matthew 16:17). Later, it would be the Holy Spirit who would help the disciples understand these things to a much greater degree (cf. John 14:26).
2. I am struck by the idea that even in his consideration of the suffering that was to come, Jesus was still consumed with bringing glory to God. Oh, that we might have that same attitude in our own sufferings.
3. Steve Jeffrey, Michael Ovey, and Andrew Sach, *Pierced for Our Transgressions: Rediscovering the Glory of Penal Substitution* (Wheaton, IL: Crossway Books, 2007), 57. The Bible version quoted is the New International Version, 1984.
4. In describing the Holy Spirit's unique empowerment for his messianic ministry, the gospel writers claim that something, in fact, was seen physically coming upon Jesus (Luke 3:22). And the best way they knew to describe it was that the Spirit's descent for empowerment was comparable to the descent of a dove. Yet in all the accounts, the metaphorical word "like" is used for purposes of comparison only (see Matthew 3:16; Mark 1:10; Luke 3:22; John 1:32).
5. Darrell Bock, *Luke 9:51–24:53: Baker Exegetical Commentary on the New Testament* (Grand Rapids, MI: Baker Books, 1996), 1761–1762.
6. For more on the use of metaphors, see Janet Soskice's *Metaphor and Religious Language* (Oxford: Clarendon, 1985). She defines *metaphor* as "a speaking of one thing in terms that are suggestive of another" (p. 49). Both similes and metaphors have similar goals as they compare two ideas or things, but a simile is different in that it adds the word *as* or *like*.
7. Kevin J. Vanhoozer defines *metaphor* as "indispensable cognitive instruments that enable thought to perceive resemblances between things that would not otherwise be observable. Metaphor is the imagination making creative connections, thinking laterally, talking out loud." Kevin J. Vanhoozer, *Is There a Meaning in This Text? The Bible* (Grand Rapids, MI: Zondervan, 1998), 129.

Chapter 38 A Footrace to the Tomb

1. Andreas J. Köstenberger remarks, "This means that the person reclining close to Jesus at the last supper in the upper room; the person providing Peter with access to the high-priestly courtyard; the person to whom care for Jesus' mother is entrusted at the foot of the cross, the person along with Peter in chapters 20 and 21; and the Fourth Evangelist (21:24; cf. 21:20) are all one and the same individual." Andreas J. Köstenberger, *John: Baker Exegetical Commentary on the New Testament* (Grand Rapids, MI: Baker Academic, 2004), 562.

2. D. A. Carson, *The Gospel According to John: Pillar New Testament Commentary* (Grand Rapids, MI: Eerdmans Publishing, 1991), 636–637, emphasis mine.

3. Carson, *The Gospel According to John: Pillar New Testament Commentary*, 637.

Chapter 39 The Romantic Wording in Song of Songs

1. Tremper Longman, *Song of Songs: New International Commentary on the Old Testament* (Grand Rapids, MI: Eerdmans Publishing, 2001), 38.

2. Longman, *Song of Songs: New International Commentary on the Old Testament*, 43.

3. See "Goat," in the *Dictionary of Biblical Imagery*, ed. Leland Ryken, James C Wilhoit, and Tremper Longman III (Downers Grove, IL: InterVarsity Press, 1998), 332.

4. A resource book to have on your shelf is the *Dictionary of Biblical Imagery* published by InterVarsity Press in 1998. It will help with grasping what a lot of these images, symbols, metaphors, and figures of speech meant in the ancient world.

5. Longman, *Song of Songs*, 59.

Chapter 40 Child Sacrifice

1. Both of these Canaanite groups were descendants of Abraham's nephew Lot, and they practiced all sorts of evil in the form of idolatry, sorcery, divination, fortune-telling, consulting mediums, etc. (see Deuteronomy 18:9–14).

2. Old Testament commentators Keil and Delitzsch remark, "The offering of his son for Moloch [Molech] took place, in all probability, during the severe oppression of Ahaz by the Syrians [Arameans], and was intended to appease the wrath of the gods, as was done by the king of the Moabites in similar circumstances (ch.3:27)." C. F. Keil and F. Delitzsch, *Commentary on the Old Testament, Vol. 3: 1 and 2 Kings, 1 and 2 Chronicles* (Peabody, MA: Hendricksen Publishers, 1996), 285.

Conclusion

1. In my opinion, the pulpit philosophy sets the tone for the whole church. If the pastor models and handles biblical texts from the pulpit with a felt-needs, topically shallow, random proof-text approach, this is the kind of culture that will be created in the church, and it will not inspire many toward deeper study.

Eric J. Bargerhuff, PhD, is the Associate Dean of Academic Affairs, Professor of Bible and Theology, and Director of the Honors Program at Trinity College of Florida. He has served in pastoral ministry for more than twenty years in churches in Ohio, Illinois, and Florida. He received his doctorate in biblical and systematic theology from Trinity Evangelical Divinity School, and he is a member of the Evangelical Theological Society (ETS). Eric's passion is to write about the interpretation and application of biblical principles for the purposes of spiritual growth and reform in the church.

Eric is the author of *The Most Misused Verses in the Bible* and *The Most Misused Stories of the Bible*. He also wrote *Love that Rescues: God's Fatherly Love in the Practice of Church Discipline*, which explores the grace and fatherly love of God that should be embodied in a church's efforts to restore a brother or sister in Christ who has gone astray.

Eric and his family live in Trinity, Florida.

More from
Eric J. Bargerhuff

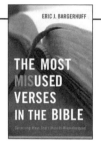

A surprising number of well-known Scripture passages are commonly misused or misunderstood. Even well-intentioned Christians take important verses out of context. In this concise yet thorough book, Eric J. Bargerhuff provides clarity in what these verses meant when they were written so we can apply them accurately today.

The Most Misused Verses in the Bible

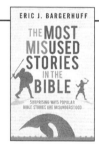

In this book, professor Eric J. Bargerhuff sheds light on 14 familiar stories that even well-intentioned Christians often misunderstand, including David and Goliath, Jonah and the Big Fish, and more. Discover the original meaning and context of each story—and its purpose for us today. Filled with fascinating historical and scriptural insights, this concise yet thorough book will help you learn how to read and apply all of God's Word more faithfully.

The Most Misused Stories in the Bible

◊BETHANYHOUSE

 Stay up to date on your favorite books and authors with our free e-newsletters. Sign up today at bethanyhouse.com.

 facebook.com/BHPnonfiction   @bethany_house_nonfiction

 @bethany_house